The Septuagint And Hebrew Chronologies Tried By The Test Of Their Internal Scientifice Evidence

THE

SEPTUAGINT AND HEBREW CHRONOLOGIES

TRIED BY THE TEST OF

THEIR INTERNAL SCIENTIFIC EVIDENCE;

WITH A TABLE FROM CREATION TO THE ACCESSION OF UZZIAH, IN B.C. 810, SHOWING THEIR JUBILEAN DIFFERENCES AT EACH DATE.

ALSO,

ON THE GREAT PERIODS

WHICH TERMINATE IN, AND MARK THE YEAR

1838,

AS THE

POINT OF TIME,

THAT SUMS UP AND CONCENTRATES AS IN A FOCUS,

THE CHRONOLOGY OF ALL PAST AGES,

AND APPEAR LIKEWISE TO SHOW, THE APPROACH OF

THE END.

By WILLIAM CUNINGHAME, Esq.

OF LAINSHAW, IN THE COUNTY OF AYR.

"BEHOLD THE LORD COMETH WITH TEN THOUSAND OF HIS SAINTS."

Enoch in Jude, ver. 14.

LONDON:

J. NISBET & CO., HATCHARD & SON, L. & G. SEELY, AND J. COCHRANE;
EDINBURGH, W. WHYTE & CO, AND W. INNES;
DUBLIN, ROBERTSON & CO.; GLASGOW, JOHN SMITH & SON.

MDCCCXXXVIII.

GLASGOW:
FULLARTON AND CO. PRINTERS, VILLAFIELD.

PREFACE.

THE question respecting the Chronology, resolves itself, as was stated by Bishop Stillingfleet, nearly two centuries ago, into a very narrow space. "The whole controversy concern-"ing this part of the Chronology of the world, (viz. from the "Deluge to Abraham,) comes at last to this: Whether it be "more probable that the Jews, who lived under the Second "Temple, (who were then the trustees, to whom were com-"mitted the *oracles of God,*) whom the LXX. followed in "their version, had the true reading, or the Talmudic Jews, "after their dispersion and banishment from their country, "when they were discarded by God himself from being his "people, when he broke up house among them at the de-"struction of Jerusalem and the Temple." *

We possess two copies of the Old Testament, the Greek and Hebrew. The former was received by us from the primitive apostolic Churches, wherein it was constantly used, and in whose assemblies it was publicly read. The latter was not in hands of the primitive apostolic Churches at all, nor was the Hebrew tongue known or studied by any of the primitive bishops till the time of Origen in the third century. There can be no question, indeed, that the Apostles themselves had the Hebrew text; but after their time, including at least a period of a century and a half to the age of Origen, it was in the exclu-

* Origines Sacræ, vol. ii. p. 150.

sive custody of the Jews, who had rejected and crucified the Messiah, and were the most virulent enemies of his Church, and from them it was received by the Church in the third and fourth centuries.

There are two passages in the Septuagint that require correction, viz., Gen. xi. 32. which now agrees with the Hebrew in making Terah die at the age of 205 instead of 145, and for the reasons which have been stated elsewhere,* the last is the true and original reading; the other is, 1 Kings vi. 1. which contains the number of 480 years, as the length of the period from the Exodus to the foundation of the Temple,† and this number, as is shown by Kennicott in a quotation from Origen, was not in the text at all in the time of that father.‡ After correcting these texts, there is a difference between the two copies, as to the age of the world, of 1474 years, arising from systematic and wilful corruptions, either in the text of the Septuagint, or the Hebrew.

Now, as the Septuagint translation of the Pentateuch was made by the Jewish Church 277 years before the Christian era, and was constantly used in the synagogues,§ and, therefore, received as authentic; and as we know, from the testimony of Demetrius, that the Chronology, which is now deduced from its text, corrected as already said, agrees even to *a year* with that which was received 220 years before Christ, it undeniably follows, that they who receive the shorter or Hebrew Chronology do really, however they may either *affect* or *choose* not to see this consequence, implicate the whole Jewish Church before our Lord's coming, in the charge of having wilfully corrupted their own Scriptures; and they further implicate the Apostles of the Lord, who always use and gener-

* See my Fulness of the Times, p. 35.

† In our copies of the LXX. the number is 440 years; but Holmes, in his edition of this version, tells us, that 4 or 5 of his MSS. read 480, and also the Complutensian edition. I, therefore, conclude 480 to have been the number originally interpolated, in conformity to the Hebrew.

‡ Kennicott, Dissert. Gener., p. 36.

§ Walton, Prolegom. ix. 37.; and Prideaux, vol. iii. pp. 63, 4. Oxford, 1830.

ally cite this version, either in the guilt of having connived at the fraud, or in the charge of ignorance of its existence.

On the contrary, we, in receiving the Chronology of the Seventy, do set our seal to the facts, that the Jewish Church, before our Lord's advent, was faithful in the preservation of the sacred text,—that the Apostles of the Lord were neither guilty of conniving at fraud, nor ignorant of the existence of fraud, but that, being inspired by the Holy Ghost, they did, in receiving the Septuagint, set their seal to the fact, that no wilful, or systematic corruption of its text, had then taken place, and, consequently, that its Chronology is true. We also charge upon the Jews, after they had rejected and crucified the Lord of glory, the awful guilt of having corrupted the whole Chronology of the Scriptures, by forged alterations in the text of Genesis and the Books of Kings, and this in order to prove, that Jesus of Nazareth had appeared too soon to be the promised Messiah, and, on the other hand, to confound and perplex *that body*, which they, of all things, hated most bitterly, namely, the Church of Christ, in its chronological calculations.

That the Jews have done these things, were there any lack of evidence of it in my former Works, and *how* they have done them, and that the Chronology of the Septuagint is the exact truth, are, I venture to affirm, placed in the following pages on the basis of demonstration. But as in the Preface of my Supplementary Dissertation I offered certain observations, which I think imbody the substance of this argument, and put certain questions to the disciples of Usher which have not been answered, I shall now again place that passage before my readers, and I again demand, from the disciples of Usher, *an answer to my questions.* And when the reader is told, that we number among the advocates of the Septuagint Chronology, Bishop Walton, the editor of the Polyglott, Kennicott, Isaac Vossius, Bishop Stillingfleet, Jackson, Hales, and many others, besides the whole primitive Church, to the age of Eusebius, and the whole Eastern Churches to the present day, who actually know nothing of the shorter Chronology, he will, I think, admit that there is no presumption on my part in putting these questions, and expecting an answer.

"It seems to me to be necessary that I should, before closing this Preface, offer a few words to allay the apprehensions of good men, whose minds are filled with fears and scruples, lest, in rejecting the Patriarchal chronology of the Hebrew text, we should shake the general authority of the Old Testament scriptures.

I observe, then, that the text of the Old Testament, used in the Apostolic churches, and by them handed down to us, was not the *Hebrew*, but the *Septuagint.*

The Rev. H. Horne, in his invaluable Introduction to the Scriptures, has accordingly shown, that of the Old Testament quotations found in the New Testament, there are, agreeing verbatim with the Septuagint, and only changing the person and number, 74; quotations from the Septuagint, with some variation, 47; agreeing with it in sense, but not in words, 32; differing from the Septuagint, but agreeing exactly or nearly with the Hebrew, 11; and differing both from the Hebrew and Septuagint, 19.*

It is plain, therefore, that the Apostles and Evangelists have given their "solemn sanction to this version."† But, according to our opponents in this argument, it contains a chronology which is false and forged. Now, either the Apostles knew this, or did not know it. If they knew it, where is their *faithfulness* in sanctioning this version? If they did not know it, where is their *inspiration?*

It is manifest that Usher and his followers do, in this question, virtually lay claim either to greater faithfulness and integrity, or to a higher gift of inspiration than the Apostles. Let them speak out and tell us plainly which; and let them forbear the censures that have sometimes been pronounced against us for precipitation and haste, till they have answered this question.

* Horne, vol. ii. p. 328—33. 7th edit.

† Ibid. p. 210.

In the next place, the Hebrew text which we now have, was not received by us from the Apostles or the Apostolic churches, but was handed to Origen and Jerome, the first of the Christian Fathers, who learned the Hebrew tongue, by the unbelieving Jews in the 3d and 4th centuries. The Christian church did, therefore, receive this text from those who, at the time, were as little the Church of God as were the Samaritans, from whom was received the Samaritan copy in the seventeenth century. Moreover, the Jews of that age had a bitterness of hostility against the cause of Christ which far exceeds their present hostility.*

It becomes therefore necessary, that the advocates of the Hebrew chronology should show us plainly upon what principle it is that they, in relation to this question, prefer the testimony of the crucifiers of the Lord of glory, the blasphemers of his name, the enemies of his Church, who had *filled up their sins alway*, as St Paul tells us, to that of the Apostles and the churches founded by them.†

But further, it is at length acknowledged by some of the ablest supporters of the Hebrew chronology, that the Jews have been actually engaged in the work of *forging* the *Scriptural chronology*, seeing that Mr Clinton gives up the number in 1 Kings vi. 1. as a forgery.‡ It is also denied by no one

* The reader is referred to my Jubilean Chronology of the Seventh Trumpet of the Apocalypse, pp. 6—12, for a more full statement of my arguments in favour of the Chronology of the Seventy.

† 1 Thess. ii. 16.

‡ *Mr Clinton has fairly given up the number of* 480 *years in this passage, and I have the happiness to accord with him respecting the whole Chronology, from the Exodus to the Foundation of the Temple, as to which our researches, though conducted separately, and in mutual ignorance of the former Works of each other, led to an* ABSOLUTE IDENTITY *of result. This being the case, the charge of rejecting and crucifying the whole testimony of the Book of Judges, which is made in* p. 89 *of the present Work, does not apply to Mr Clinton, with regard to whose Works the only sentiments I desire to express, are those of deep and unfeigned respect for their profound learning, and sincere regret to differ from their author on any question.*—N.B. This Note belongs to the present Preface, and, to distinguish it, is placed in Italic.

that the Jews have, in their Seder Olam,* corrupted the chronology of history, with a view of disproving the fulfilment of Daniel's prophecy of the seventy weeks in our Lord. These things do, therefore, utterly impugn the authority and credit of the Jewish testimony, as to the Patriarchal chronology, even as the credit of the testimony of one who has once perjured himself is for ever after destroyed.

Finally, It is so far from being the case that the reception of the Greek chronology weakens our faith in the inspiration of the Old Testament, and the general fidelity of the Hebrew text, that the direct contrary is the case. The author of this Treatise must say, that his veneration for the sacred volume has never been so profound, and his conviction of the entireness of its inspiration so deep, as since his eyes were opened to see the wonders of this chronology.—Nor does he stand alone in these feelings. It is now at length made evident, also, that no one can meddle with the sacred text, in the way of corrupting it, and hope that the corruption shall escape detection and being exposed in the face of day.

One thing, however, the author has felt, that he has not embraced that side of the question which is *popular in the Church* in the present day; but he would consider it to be purchasing the favour of his brethren at much too high and precious a price to give what he believes to be sacred and most important truth for it."

In conclusion, let it be remembered that the Church of God, from Adam to the second coming of Christ, is ONE BODY. To this body, called by St Paul *the ground and pillar of the truth,* God has committed the whole of truth that He hath seen meet to reveal to man, to be kept and used for his glory, —and of this truth, the knowledge of the times of the Church and of the World is an important part. If, then, through the negligence of the Church in past ages, this part of the truth has been lost, as has confessedly been the case from the Apostolic times, since when no two writers have agreed upon it,

* Their popular Work on Chronology.

then it is the duty of the Church, and God will require it of her, to seek for this precious pearl of wisdom with the most unremitting diligence till it is found; and, if the author of this treatise is guilty of undue presumption in expressing his belief that it *is* at length found, surely those disciples of the Hebrew Chronology, who pretend that they have put on the panoply of truth, will feel no difficulty in overthrowing his reasoning and meeting the body of facts which he has placed before them. But they must be met by *facts* and *evidence*, and not, as they have sometimes been, by *assertions*, unsupported by evidence; and if they cannot be thus met, then the inevitable conclusion must be, that the Septuagint Chronology is true, and that the upholders of the Hebrew, have been unwittingly OPPOSING THE TRUTH OF GOD.

In conclusion, I shall inform the reader that there will be found in the Appendix to Chap. I., an explanation of certain apparent discrepancies between two passages of this Work, and an omission in p. 16. of an important Hebrew era will be found supplied in the same Appendix, p. 117. Also in Appendix to Chap. II., a mistake as to the arithmetical properties of the number from the birth of Shem to the present year, being 5152 years, will be found rectified, and that period will be proved to be much more complete and comprehensive, and therefore adding more important aid and irrefragable strength to my argument than I have stated it to be in p. 91.

LAINSHAW, *October 4th*, (15 *Tisri*) 1838.

POSTSCRIPT TO THE PREFACE.

Since the Appendix to Chapter I. was sent to the Press, I have discovered that the Hebrew date of the death of Cainan, B.C. 2769, is also taken from the Greek Chronology. It is from the death of Seth in the Septuagint, B.C. 4337, 32 Jubilees, and 2 Jubilees from the death of Noah, B.C. 2867. Also, from this Hebrew era to the birth of Jacob, B.C. 1985, in the Greek are 16 Jubilees, and to the 1st Passover in the Second Temple, B.C. 515, are 46 Jubilees,—the last date being common to the two Chronologies. This date is also a part of the Series of Metonic Cycles from the Hebrew era of Creation, or in the Greek, the 2d year current of Lamech, B.C. 4004, being from it 65 Cycles, and thence to the death of Jacob, B.C. 1838, are 49 Cycles, or 19 Jubilees.

I have, moreover, found that the Hebrew date of the death of Jared, B.C. 2582, belongs to the Greek Jubilean Series of 105 Jubilees, or 15 Cubes of 7 from the birth of Japhet to the year 1829, when, by the passing of the Catholic Emancipation Act, Great Britain ceased to be a Protestant kingdom. The above Hebrew date is from B.C. 3317, the Greek date of the birth of Japhet 15 Jubilees; and thence, viz. B.C. 2582, to the taking of Jerusalem by David, B.C. 1063, are 31 Jubilees. These new evidences of the craft of the Jewish Rabbis confirm the remarks which will be found in page 120, showing that the whole structure of their curtailed system was formed on the basis of the scientific periods of the true Chronology.

I shall now place before the reader some further direct evidence of the truth of the Septuagint Chronology, discovered by me also since the Appendixes were printed:—

1. From the birth of Mahalaleel, B.C. 4684, reckoning the Cycle of $1040 \times 3 = 3120$ years, we arrive at B.C. 1564, the beginning of the administration of Othniel, and, therefore, the epoch of the Judges; whence, to the present year, 1838, are 179 Cycles of 19, subdivided, as mentioned in page 71.

This great Series of Cyclical time, therefore, brings the birth of Mahalaleel into the number of the great eras with which the year 1838 is connected.

2. From the death of Jared, B.C. 3557, computing 1040 years, we arrive at B.C. 2517, the beginning of the administration of Eber, distinguished as a great era in the Series of Metonic Cycles from the birth of Enos. See page 18.

3. From the birth of Peleg, B.C. 2686, reckoning 2 Cycles of 1040 = 2080, we arrive at B.C. 606, the era of the captivity in Babylon.

4. From the same date, reckoning the Cycle of 2262 years, the Moon fast 14 H., 53 M., we arrive at B.C. 424, the era of the finishing of the Old Testament Canon, and death of Artaxerxes Longimanus, and thence to the next year, 1839, is the same period of 2262 years.

5. Finally, from the birth of Ham, B.C. 3314, to the year A.C. 1792, the epoch of the Seventh Trumpet of the Apocalypse, and end of Daniel's 2300 and 1260 years, are 5105 years, a Cycle composed of that of $334 \times 10 = 3340 + 353 \times 5 = 1765$ years, the Moon slow at the end of it, 3 H., 49 M., 46 S., 20 TH.; and the former subdivision of it, or 3340 years, leads us to the year A.C. 27, the beginning of the ministry of John the Baptist, and opening of the Gospel dispensation, even as the year 1792 is the opening of the dispensation of Judgment on the Fourth Beast of Daniel.

October 13*th*, 1838.

I add, for the sake of unlearned persons, an Explanation of Signs and Abbreviations used in this Work.

$+$ *plus*, or *more*, the sign of Addition;	thus $2 + 2$, is equal to 4.
$-$ *minus*, or *less*, the sign of Subtraction;	thus $6 - 2$, is equal to 4.
$\times$ The sign of Multiplication;	thus 3×3, is equal to 9.
$\div$ The sign of Division;	thus $9 \div 3$, is equal to 3.
$=$ The sign of Equality;	thus $3 \times 3 = 9$.

The letters B.C. mean *Before Christ*, or the years *before* the vulgar era of the *Nativity*, or *Birth of Christ*, which is 3 years later than the true date of his birth. He was therefore born, B.C. (Before Christ) 3.

A.C. means *After Christ*, or years *after* the vulgar era of his Birth.

7^2, or 5^2, means the Square of $7 = 49$, or of $5 = 25$.

7^3, or 5^3, means the Cube of $7 = 343$, or of $5 = 125$.

CONTENTS.

SECTION II.

CHAPTER II.

ERRATA.

The reader is requested to be so kind as correct the errata before reading the Work:—

Page 7, line 6 from bottom, for 92, read 82.
—— 44, line 1, erase the full stop after *subdivisions*.
—— 46, column of events, line 12, erase the semicolon after *Canaan*, and place it in line 13, after *events*.
—— 93, line 2, for 1838, read 1839.
—— — line 4, for *this*, read *that*.
—— 106, column of names after Jeroboam in Israel, for 23, read 22.
—— 112, column of events, last line, for 1835, read 1335.
—— 112, column of Dates above the year 1868, insert *After Christ*.

As my *Synopsis of Chronology* is closely connected with this Work, I shall add that, since its publication, the columns of *Years of the World*, and *Before* and *After Christ*, have been carefully examined, and the only error detected in them is the transposition of two figures in p. 79, Y. W. 5419 instead of 5149. In the column of events, page 87, line 11 from the bottom, 532 is misprinted for 132; in p. 88, in the same column, line 15 from bottom, 54 for 254.—In the text, p. 35, there are two errors of addition, 6811 and 6830 for 5811 and 5830.—In the note, p. 75, line 10, *artem* is misprinted for *autem*. In p. 98, column of events, under the head of *Eastern Empire*, for *Stauvacius* read *Stauracius*. In the column of Names, p. 122, insert the name of "*Anne*" opposite *Queen of England*. It appears to have been drawn accidentally out of the page when at Press, as it is in one copy in my possession. In p. 125, Clement IX. ought to be Clement XIV. I shall also add, that two errors of dates, in a Note in p. iv. of the Preface, and a misprint of *Darius* for *David*, rendered it necessary to reprint that leaf. Purchasers, in whose copies *Darius* is printed in that page, will be entitled to receive corrected copies from their Booksellers in exchange for their present copies, *without charge*.

SECOND POSTSCRIPT TO THE PREFACE.

I FIND that the following great periods are yet to be added to those coming out in 1838:—

	DATES. Years A.C.	INTERVALS to 1838.	REMARKS.
The 1st Passover after the sale of the lands of Judea to strangers, and the Epoch of the final dispersion of the Jewish nation,	74	1764	36 Jubilees, or 12 × 3, a perfect period.
The defeat of the insurgent Saxons by the Generals of Charlemagne, and the entire subjection of Saxony, according to Sismondi, Hist. des Français, Tome ii. p. 364-5,	798	1040	A perfect Cycle, the Moon slow 1 H. 18 M. 8 S. 19 TH.
The preaching of the Crusade against the Albigenses, according to Sismondi, ib. Tome vi. p. 607-8, and the Abbé Millot, Hist. Moderne, Tome ii. p. 146,	1208	630	The perfect Cycle of 315 years × 2, the Moon fast 6 H. 1 M. 33 S. 4 TH.
The accession of Henry VII. of England, and the union of the houses of York and Lancaster,	1485	353	A perfect Cycle, the Moon fast 1 H. 7 M. 24 S. 38 TH.

All these the intelligent reader will perceive are great Eras of History.

October 23d, 1838.

CORRECTION IN THE ERRATA.

Erase the 3d of the former Errata, and for it read as follows:—
Page 46, column of Events, line 12, for the *semicolon* after *Canaan* insert a *comma*, and place a *semicolon* in line 13 after *Greek*.

THE

SEPTUAGINT AND HEBREW CHRONOLOGIES,

&c.

CHAPTER I.

THE SEPTUAGINT AND HEBREW CHRONOLOGIES TRIED BY THE TEST OF THEIR INTERNAL SCIENTIFIC EVIDENCE.

SECTION I.

MY argument for the Septuagint Chronology, founded upon its scientific structure, has been sometimes met by the assertions, that it is possible, in any scheme of time, to find Jubilean and other scientific periods,—and that, in point of fact, such periods distinguish the shorter or Hebrew no less than the longer or Greek Chronology.

It is not necessary that I should deny the truth of the former assertion; indeed, it would be in vain to deny it, seeing it must be obvious to every understanding, that in every possible scheme of time covering the records of history, any given year must be connected with certain other years by Jubilean and Cyclical intervals. This is a chronological truism. Let it be observed, therefore, that the question really to be decided, is not whether every scheme of mundane time must contain Jubilean and Cyclical periods; but whether in any scheme but the one ordained by the Creator, we shall find all the great periods of the world, measured in comely order and harmonious proportions by scientific time; and by this term I request my readers to understand, 1st, the *Cycles of Astronomy;* and 2dly, those periods of which the bases are the *perfect numbers*, 7 and 12, and also 5 and 10, either multiplied by themselves or by one another; and 3d, such numbers as are the *squares* or *cubes* of others, as 4, 8, 27, &c.; and 4th, numbers which are the *sums* of other perfect numbers, as 17, the sum of 7 and 10. Now, since it is self-evident that no supposable arrangement of the times of the INTELLIGENT UNIVERSE, except that which is the contrivance of an INFINITE UNDERSTANDING, can in the nature of things exhibit the features of perfect order, seeing that such an arrangement is itself the demonstration, of that infallible foreknowledge and almighty power, which are the incommunicable attributes of the Godhead, it appears undeniably to follow, that if we can discover such a scheme, it must at once commend itself to us by the evidence of its internal structure, as the authentic Chronology contrived and ordained by the Creator. For if the makers of our finest chronometers, do upon their almost perfect workmanship, stamp the indelible evidences of their mechanical science, surely it were a derogation from the glorious attributes of Him, who made all things, to affirm that his great chronometer of the ages of the Moral Universe, as the order of time ordained by Him may fitly be called, shall, when discovered, be without the plainest demonstrations of his omniscience and almighty power.

With respect next to the assertion, that the shorter or Hebrew Chronology actually exhibits a scientific and Jubilean arrangement no less than the Greek, I have already shown in my Fulness of the Times,* that the Hebrew Doctors must have possessed a thorough knowledge of the Jubilean arrangement of the SACRED TIMES, and that they have, in curtailing them, used their utmost endeavours to preserve their Jubilean

* Chapter V.

character, which they have in part effected. I must, however, add, that when that Work was written, I was far from perceiving how deep have been their artifices for this end.

In order that the reader may see, at one view, the mode in which the Jubilean relations have been, as far as possible, preserved, in corrupting the Chronology, I shall place in this work* a comparative table of the two schemes, from Creation to the accession of Uzziah, when they meet at a common point, B.C. 810,—there being no important difference between them from that date to the Christian era,—and in the two last columns is exhibited their exact difference in Years and Jubilees, at each date; whereby it will be clearly seen that the corruption was effected with the settled purpose of preserving the Jubilean character of the Chronology.—This is done by curtailing it, as nearly as possible, by complete Jubilees or Septenaries, at all the great eras of time in the primitive patriarchal ages, from which the great Jubilean series of the original Chronology are reckoned; the result of which is, that in bringing down streams of Jubilees from the same eras in the Chronology, whether in the Greek or Hebrew schemes, to ages posterior to the Christian era, they arrive at points of time differing from each other, only so far as the amount of variation between the two schemes at the commencement of each series is short of a complete Jubilean number.

It will, accordingly, be seen that the difference between the Chronologies at the era of Creation, is exactly 30 Jubilees and 4 years; that at the birth and death of Enos it is 26 Jubilees and only 1 year; at the birth and death of Cainan, 23 Jubilees and 48 years, or only 1 year less than 24 Jubilees; and at the birth of Eber, in B. C. 2820, according to the Seventy, and B. C. 2281, according to the Hebrew, the two Chronologies differ exactly 539 years, or 11 Jubilees; so that a series of Jubilees brought down from either date will exactly coincide, from the first Jubilee after the Hebrew date of his birth, to the end of time.

* See the Table at the end.

At first view it must be confessed that this circumstance of the near approximation of the two Chronologies, and in the period from the birth of Eber, their exact agreement, in Jubilean series, appears to be of a perplexing nature, and calculated to increase the difficulties which environ the whole of this inquiry; but, upon a more close examination, I have found that it affords greater facilities in analyzing both systems—and for distinguishing the original from the corrupt Chronology—and establishing the former with a weight of evidence, which will, I think, be found irresistible by every candid mind.

I shall proceed to show the truth of what has now been advanced by an inquiry into both schemes, at some of the various points of time where their differences are nearly Jubilean, beginning with the era of Creation.

The difference between the Greek and Hebrew eras of Creation, the former being B.C. 5478, and the latter B.C. 4004, is 1474 years, equal to 30 Jubilees and 4 years. Consequently, as it has been shown in my Synopsis of Chronology that in the former Chronology a series of $12 \times 12 = 144$ Jubilees, computed from the era of Creation, comes out in the year 1579, the date of the Union of Utrecht,* it follows that in the Hebrew Chronology a series of 114 Jubilees, or 294 Cycles of 19, comes out 4 years later, viz., in 1583: And as this period unites in itself the Jubilee and Metonic Cycle, being either 6 Jubilees of Cycles, or 6 Cycles of Jubilees, it is a perfect one; but it terminates in a year not marked by any signal events, and therefore no era of history.—In the next place, as from Creation, B.C. 5478, to the year 1824, there are in the Septuagint Chronology exactly 149 Jubilees, so there are in the Hebrew, from Creation, B.C. 4004, to the year 1828, a period of 119 Jubilees, being 7×17, or 17 cubes of 7; and as 17 is one of the numbers most frequently found in the Scriptural series, this period is a perfect one.—If also we add 1 year to it, we arrive at 1829, and have a period of 5832 years from the Usherite era of Creation to that year, being

* Synopsis, p. 29. The reader will be pleased, in that place, to correct the error in figures opposite 144 ;—for 7066 read 7056.

exactly 40½ squares of 12. The two years, 1828 and 1829, where these great periods expire, are also marked and important eras. In the former the last war between Russia and Turkey began. In the latter it was concluded by a peace, leaving Turkey a tributary power, and establishing also the independence of Greece. In this year, moreover, was passed the Catholic Emancipation Bill, demolishing the Protestant constitution of Great Britain by the admission of the Romanists into the high places of power.

It will, in the next place, be found, that reckoning from Usher's era of Creation a series of 305 Metonic Cycles, being 2 cubes, 2 squares, and the root of the sacred number 5, it comes out in 1792, the era of the Seventh Trumpet of the Apocalypse, and the termination of the 2300 and 1260 years of Daniel; and adding to it 3 Cycles, it becomes 308, or $19 \times 7 \times 11 = 1463 \times 4 = 5852$ years, ending in the year 1849.

If, then, it will be said, it be so, that both schemes of Chronology, the Hebrew as well as the Greek, are thus found to contain great and perfect periods of scientific time, marking leading eras of the world, how are we to distinguish between them, and to determine which is the original and which the corrupted Chronology? To this we answer, that the true Chronology being the order of time ordained of God, and the false the mutilation of that order, the former must, when minutely analyzed, like all the other works of the Creator, bear traces of his infinite wisdom, inimitable by any forged or corrupted scheme of time; and it will be found so in the present instance. Yet, on the other hand, the false Chronology being not a pure invention, but the corruption of the truth, and having been devised by persons who were well acquainted with the principles of the true Chronology, may be expected to have retained traces of some of its features of order and scientific harmony. It is only, therefore, as already said, by a *minute analysis*, that we can arrive at a satisfactory solution of this question, and that the true is to be certainly distinguished from the false.

In entering on this analysis, I shall begin by a review of the series of Jubilees from the Greek era of Creation, B. C. 5478.—At the end of 91, being 13 weeks of Jubilees or cubes of 7 = 4459 years, this series arrives at B. C. 1019, the dedication of the first Temple. Thence 21 Jubilees, or 3 cubes of 7, make from Creation the number of 5088 years, being 7 × 4 = 28 × 4 = 112 Jubilees, or the cube of 7 × 16, and bring us to the year A. C. 11, when Christ entered his 14th year, the age of puberty, at which boys under the law were subject to ordinances; and, therefore, at this point of time our Lord first appeared *in his own person.* Carrying on the series to 1530, it is 11 × 13 = 143 Jubilees; and in that year the Protestant Confession of Augsburg was presented to the Emperor Charles V., and having been read before him and the assembled Princes of the Empire at Augsburg, was published throughout Europe. The confederacy of Smalcalde was formed the same year. Next, at the end of 144 Jubilees, being the square of 7 = 49 multiplied by the square of 12, this series arrives at 1579, the era of the union of Utrecht, which was the foundation of the Dutch Republic; and thereby was finished the number of the States of Europe, embracing the Reformation. Four Jubilees more, being 148 from Creation, bring us to the year 1775, the beginning of the American war, which was the precursor of the French Revolution. The 149th Jubilee terminated in 1824, when also a period of 1260 years × 4 = 5040 from the Deluge, came out, each of the parts of which touches important eras; the first 1260 arrives at B. C. 1957, Jacob's 28th year complete; the second at B. C. 697, the date of the death of Hezekiah and accession of Manasseh; the third 1260 reaches the year A. C. 564, the last of Justinian. The year 1824 was distinguished by the death of Louis XVIII. and the accession of Charles IX., the last of the elder branch of the Bourbons, also by the further progress of the Greek arms, which gave them possession of Napoli di Romania and other places. The first Septenary of years of this Jubilee having been filled with stupendous events, ended in 1831, exactly 200 Cycles of 19 from the death of Abraham, in which year the army of Egypt entered Palestine, occupied Jerusalem, and laid siege to Acra; and the Reform Bill was brought in, and Parliament having been dissolved, a new Parliament was elected under the influence of revolutionary terror. The 150th Jubilee from Creation did thus usher in the events of THE END.

In the next place, calculating from the Hebrew era of Creation, B. C. 4004, a series of Jubilees, I find that the important eras in Usher's Chronology of the Old Testament which are touched by it are, 1st, the date of the conception of Methuselah, B. C. 3318, being 686 years, or 14 Jubilees, from the Creation; and it is worthy of observation that, in the Greek Chronology, the same year, B. C. 3318, is the date of the conception of Japhet, 14 Jubilees from the 2d year of Lamech, B. C. 4004. The 2d era in this series of Usher is his date of the Covenant of Circumcision, and of the conception of Isaac and destruction of Sodom, and it is from Creation 43 Jubilees, an imperfect period. The same events are, in the Greek, placed in B. C. 2046, which is 70 Jubilees and 2 years from Creation, in that Chronology. The 3d era in Usher is his date of the accession of Solomon, B. C. 1015, which is from Creation, in his scheme, 61 Jubilees or 2989 years. 4th, At the end of 82 Jubilees or 4018 years from Creation, this series arrives at the year A. C. 15, when, according to Usher, Christ was in his 19th year; but, according to my Chronology, his 18th.—Let it, however, be observed, that the 19th year of Christ is not a legal period of his age, as is his 14th, when under the LAW he first appeared in his own person, at which time, in the Greek Chronology, a period of 112 Jubilees, or 16 Cubes of 7 from Creation, comes to an end. Moreover, with the exception of the first, of 14 Jubilees, the other periods, namely, 43, 61, and 92 Jubilees, in this series of Usher, are all imperfect, not being divisible by 5, or 7, or 12, and single Jubilean periods are inadmissible in a series beginning from Creation. It is not till we carry on this series to the middle ages of our era, and arrive at the year of Christ 1485, the date of the accession of Henry VII. of England, and of the union of the Houses of York and Lancaster, that we attain in it to the perfect period of 112 Jubilees. Now let the reader decide which of these events as the termination of that great and perfect period, which is, as it were, imbosomed in the name of Jehovah himself, since the Hebrew letters for JEHOVAH ELOHIM, contain exactly the number 112,* bears upon it the stamp of that Divine skill and workmanship which have formed the times and seasons according to the principles of his eternal wisdom. Is the 14th year of Messiah, the SECOND ADAM, and the date of his first personal appearance, seeing that he before appeared simply as the child of Joseph and Mary, and, as it were, in their persons and not his own, or the accession of Henry VII. of England! the event most likely to illustrate the end of a great and perfect period of four times four cubes of 7, from the creation of the FIRST ADAM? And is that scheme of time which brings to pass the former result, or the one which brings out the latter, from the Creator?

Nor is there in the Jewish opinion that the number 112, which is contained in the letters of the DIVINE NAME, was, when multiplied by the Jubilee, to bring the Messiah into the world, any thing which is alien from our conceptions of the power and wisdom of God. It is, on the contrary, in entire harmony with all his glorious perfections, that the very letters of the name of the Creator should, in the sacred and primitive tongue, reveal to his church the deep things of wisdom, and the times and seasons of that great mystery of godliness, GOD MANIFEST IN THE FLESH, and the season of his Advent.

* The number is thus made out:

י	10		א	1
ה	5		ל	30
ו	6		ה	5
ה	5		י	10
			ם	40
	26	+		86 = 112.

The arithmetical power of these letters depends on their position in the Hebrew alphabet, and if we believe, as even the Heathen did, that letters were given by revelation, then the order of the alphabet and arithmetical power of *these letters* were *directly from God.*

As it may, however, be thought by some, that the series of Jubilees from the Hebrew date of Creation, does at least contain some show of plausibility, inasmuch as it touches (though not, be it again observed, by a perfect period) the year of the accession of Solomon, I shall now inform the reader that there is, in the Septuagint Chronology, a better and more perfect series from the same date, B. C. 4004, which, in that scheme, is the 2d year of Lamech, who was born B. C. 4005.

	Dates. Years B. C.	Intervals. Years.	Jubilees.	Remarks.
The 2d year of Lamech.	4004			
The year before the birth of Japhet, being that of his conception.	3318	686	14	2 Cubes of 7.
The second year of Isaac.	2044	1274	26	From the 2d of Lamech, the perfect period of 40 Jubilees.
The 2d year of the Administration of Ehud.	1505	539	11	Being 7 + 4, and a number constantly found in the Scripture Chronology, as the measure of intermediate periods.
The 2d year of that of Gideon.	1358	147	3	These 2 periods make 14 Jubilees, or 2 cubes of 7 from the 2d of Isaac.
David's last year in Hebron.	1064	294	6	This era is 60 Jubilees from the 2d of Lamech. It will be shown in another series that it is 20 Squares of 12, from the death of the 1st Cainan.
The 16th year of Solomon's reign.	1015	49	1	
The last vision of Ezekiel.	574	441	9	The whole series from the 2d of Lamech, is 70 Jubilees.

Now, by comparing these two Series in the Hebrew and and Greek Chronologies, it will be made evident to the attentive reader, and none but attentive and diligent readers ought to meddle with this subject, that in the former, all the intervals are, with the exception of that to the conception of Methuselah, imperfect, while in the Greek they are perfect. The simple fact seems to have been, that this series of 70 Jubilees, from the 2d year of Lamech to B. C. 574, when Ezekiel saw his last vision, having marked the former year, as a great era; the Scribes have, in curtailing the Chronology, assumed it as a convenient date of Creation, and have cut down the whole series of time accordingly; but though they have preserved the period of 70 Jubilees, yet in filling it up, they have utterly failed in preserving its original internal evidences of symmetry and perfect order.

For the purpose, however, of establishing beyond all controversy the spuriousness and falsehood of the Hebrew date of Creation, and the truth of the Greek era, it becomes necessary to apply to both the test of the Metonic Cycle. We have already seen that, from the Hebrew date, B.C. 4004, a series of 305 Cycles terminates in 1792, the date of the fall of the French monarchy, and of the great war of the Revolution. But in carrying on this series through the intervening ages, I can, in the system of Usher, discover no traces whatever of a Mundane Chronology founded on the Cycle of 19. Indeed, I have not found, computing either by weeks of 19 = 133, or the square of 19 = 361, that this series does, in the Chronology of Usher, touch a single intermediate date of importance. But in the Greek Chronology we have, from the 2d year of Lamech, B.C. 4004, to the death of Jacob, B.C. 1838, the period of 114 Cycles, or 6 Squares of 19, and thence to 1792, are 191 Cycles; or to 1811, the last year of the prosperity of Napoleon and his unbroken power, 192, or 16 twelves of 19. In the Hebrew scheme, however, the year B. C. 1838 is distinguished by no event, and is not marked as an era at all, being just 8 years after the death of Shem. Even this Series, founded on the Hebrew Chronology, does, therefore, when minutely analyzed, afford new evidence of the authenticity of the Greek.

Turning next to the era of Creation according to the Septuagint, B.C. 5478, I proceed to demonstrate, that the whole times of the church and the world, computed from that year, are most artificially arranged on the basis of the Cycle of 19. The evidence of this will be found in the following Table:—

EVENTS.	DATES. Years B.C.	INTERVALS. Years.	Cycles of 19.	REMARKS.
1. The Creation,	5478			
2. The birth of Enoch,	4357	1121	59	From the birth of Enoch to the flood are 12 × 5 = 60 Cycles, and to the death of Christ there are 231 Cycles, being 7 × 11 = 77 × 3, or 33 weeks of that Cycle, and both are perfect periods.
3. The deluge,	3217	1140	60	The Flood is from Creation 7 × 17 = 119 Cycles, a perfect period. Thence to the death of Christ are 9 Squares of 19.
4. Babel founded,	2400	817	43	My reasons for fixing this date, and the evidence which supports it, will be found in the Preface to the Synopsis of Chronology, pp. xviii–xxii. and I think it will commend itself to the mind of the judicious reader as altogether conclusive. This and the date of the death of Joshua are the only two eras in Old Testament times in this Series, which are not directly supported by Scriptural testimony, and I have omitted the death of Joshua.
5. Jacob arrives at Shechem, and erects an altar called EL-ELOHE-ISRAEL. This is a great Scriptural era,	1887	513	27	Being 27, the cube of 3, and one of the numbers which most frequently measure the intermediate periods in the Scriptural Chronology. The whole interval, from the Flood to this era, is 70 Cycles, or 10 weeks of 19, a most perfect number; and from Creation the period is 27 weeks of the Cycle of 19. In my Synopsis, p. 142, I placed this event in the same year as Jacob's return from Padan-aram. The Targum of Jonathan, however, concludes from the words of Gen. xxxiii. 17. that he remained at Succoth a whole year. I think there is reason to acquiesce in this conclusion, and it places his arrival at Shechem in the year following.

Events.	Dates. Years B.C.	Intervals. Years.	Intervals. Cycles of 19.	Remarks.
6. The 3d year of the Servitude of Moses,	1678	209	11	This era is from Creation 200 Cycles; from the Deluge 9 × 9 = 81; and from the foundation of Babel, 2 Squares of 19.
7. God appears to Moses at the Bush,	1640	38	2	From the Flood 83 Cycles, and the foundation of Babel 40. This era bisects the whole period from the Flood to the taking of Jerusalem by Pompey.
8. The 3d year of Saul's reign,	1108	532	28	Being 7 × 4, or 4 weeks of the Cycle of 19. The 3d year of Saul is particularly marked in the Scriptures. (See 1 Sam. xiii. 1.) All the events recorded in that and the following chapters, are to be placed in this year, though Usher has, without any warrant for it, made an interval of 6 years between them. It was at this time that Saul, properly speaking, took the kingdom over Israel. (I Sam. xiv. 47.) This era is, from Creation, 230 Cycles; from the birth of Enoch, 171 Cycles, or 9 Squares of 19. Thence to the death of Christ, are 60 Cycles.
9. The accession of David,	1070	38	2	His accession is from the foundation of Babel, 70 Cycles; from Jacob's arrival at Shechem, 43; from the appearance of God to Moses, 30.
10. The era of Nabonassar,	747	323	17	This great era being the proper beginning of Daniel's first kingdom, is from Creation, . . Cycles. 249 The birth of Enoch 10 Squares of 19 = . . 190 The Deluge, . . . 130 Jacob's arrival at Shechem 12 × 5 = . 60 The 3d year of Moses' Servitude, 19 Jubilees, or 7 × 7 = ... 49 The 3d year of Saul 1 Square of 19, . . . 19 All these periods are complete.

Events.	Dates. Years B.C.	Intervals. Years.	Cycles of 19.	Remarks.
11. Babylon taken by Cyrus,	538	209	11	The taking of Babylon is, from Creation, (Cycles.) 260 From the foundation of Babel, 7 × 14 = 98 or 38 Jubilees. From the 3d year of the Servitude of Moses, 60 From the 3d of Saul, 30 The accession of David, 28 The taking of Babylon also bisects the whole period from the death of Noah, B.C. 2867, to the year 1792, when the 1260 years of Daniel and St John expired.
12. The death of Artaxerxes Longimanus, and, (according to Josephus, against Apion,) the completion of the Old Testament Canon,	424	114	6	This great era is from Creation 14 Squares of 19 years, and from the Deluge, 147 = 7 × 21 Cycles, or 57 Jubilees; and as this number unites in itself the Metonic Cycle and Jubilee, both periods are perfect. It is from Jacob's arrival at Shechem, 7 × 11 = ... (Cycles.) 77 From the appearance to Moses at the Bush, 8 × 8 = ... 64 The 3d year of Saul, 12 × 3 = ... 36 The 1st of David, 17 × 2 = ... 34 All these periods are complete.
13. The complete subjection of Persia by Alexander the Great, and death of the Usurper Bessus, which is the end of Daniel's SECOND kingdom, and era of the establishment of the THIRD,	329	95	5	Being from the Deluge 8 Squares of 19, and before the death of Christ, 1 Square.
14. Jerusalem taken by Pompey, and the Holy of Holies profaned, which is the epoch of the dominion of Daniel's FOURTH kingdom over the Church of God,	63	266	14	Being from the end of Persia 2 weeks of 19 years,—from the end of the Old Testament Canon, 1 Square of 19,—from the Creation, 15 Squares of 19,—and from the Deluge, 166 Cycles, which period is bisected by the appearance of God to Moses at Horeb.

Events.	Dates. Years A.C.	Intervals. Years.	Cycles of 19.	Remarks.
15. The death, resurrection, and ascension, of Christ,	33	95	5	From Creation 290 Cycles,—from the birth of Enoch 33 weeks of Cycles,—from the Deluge 9 squares of 19,—from the appearance of God to Moses 88 Cycles, or 11 × 8,—from the 3d of Saul 60,—from the taking of Babylon 30,—from the end of the Old Testament Canon 24 Cycles,—from the end of Persia 1 square of 19. All these are complete periods.
16. Theodosius the Great for the last time unites the whole Roman Empire under his sceptre for one year,	394	361	19	Being 1 square of 19. Cycles. From Creation, 309 The birth of Enoch, 250 The Flood 10 squares of 19, ... 190 The foundation of Babel 57 Jubilees, or 147 Jacob's arrival at Shechem, ... 120 The accession of David 7 × 11, ... 77 The era of Nabonassar 12 × 5, ... 60 The taking of Babylon 19 Jubilees, ... 49 The end of Persia 2 squares of 19, . . . 38 The taking of Jerusalem by Pompey, . . 24
17. The siege of Rome, by Astolphus and the Lombards, raised a second time by Pepin, mayor of the palace of France, who gives possession to the Pope of several towns, and next year cedes to him the Exarchate. This is the epoch of the temporal power of the Pope,	755	361	19	Cycles. From Creation, 328 From the Flood 11 squares of 19, . . . 209 From the accession of David 12 × 8, . . . 96 From the end of Persia 3 squares of 19, . . 57 From the death of Christ 2 squares, . . 38
18. Maximilian of Austria marries Mary, heiress of Charles the Bold, killed this year at the siege of Nancy. This marriage is the keystone of the arch of the whole modern politics of Continental Europe. The issue of this marriage was Philip of Austria, who, 19 years afterwards, viz. in 1496, married Joan the foolish, heiress of the Spanish monarchy; and their first-born son was Charles V. of Germany, in 1500.	1477	722	38	Or 2 squares of 19. From the Flood 13 squares of 19. From the death of Christ 4 squares.

Events.	Dates. Years A.C.	Intervals. Years.	Cycles of 19.	Remarks.
19. The year	1838	361	19	The year 1838 is from Creation 385 Cycles of 19, being 20 squares of that number, and 5 Cycles, or 55 weeks of 19. But as its relation to the whole Chronology of the world will be treated of afterwards, I shall not now enlarge upon it.

It will be seen that the foregoing stupendous series comprehends in it all the leading eras of history, the Creation, the Deluge, the appearance of God to Moses, which was the beginning of the dispensation of the law—the accession of David—the beginning of the first, second, and third kingdoms of Daniel, and of the dominion of the fourth kingdom over the church of God—the death, resurrection, and ascension of our Lord, and the beginning of the temporal power of the Pope. If, moreover, the reader will carefully analyze the whole numbers, he will find, besides the various examples of the *Septenary*, or *twelves* of the Cycle, measuring important periods, that the square of 19 enters into the whole Chronology; but as this will be brought before the reader in treating of the Chronology of the year 1838, I forbear entering upon it here. Now, as it is utterly impossible that a false or forged Chronology, which was confessedly in existence 200 years before Christ, should have imbodied in it results which so manifestly mark the superintending care of a wisdom and contrivance above that of the creature, the inevitable consequence is, that the scheme of time containing these results is not false, as is asserted by the disciples of Usher, but is the exact truth; and that of the Hebrew text, which contains no similar results, is a corruption of the truth. Another argument for this is, that part of the foregoing series of Chronology, viz. from the era of Nabonassar to the present year, is common to both schemes, and therefore in both, we have from that era, the same series of Metonic Cycles; but while in the Greek, it ascends up to Creation, in the Hebrew it utterly fails, if carried higher than the era of Nabonassar. That Chronology, wherein the series ascends up to the beginning, must therefore be the original, and the scheme wherein it suddenly stops at the year B. C. 747, must be spurious and corrupt. Moreover, it is agreeable to analogy, that a series which touches the eras of the death and ascension to heaven of Christ, of Daniel's four kingdoms, and the taking of Babylon and Jerusalem, which this one does, both in the Greek and Hebrew schemes, should begin at the Creation, and touch the Deluge also. Now, it does this in the Greek but not in the Hebrew, therefore the Greek and not the Hebrew is the original. I feel utterly at a loss to conceive, in what manner the advocates of the Hebrew Chronology, are to evade the force of this argument.

It has been seen in a former page, that at another great era in sacred history, viz. the birth of Enos, according to the Septuagint, B. C. 5044, and the Hebrew, B. C. 3769, the difference between the two schemes to the Christian era is 1275 years, being 26 Jubilees and 1 year, and also 67 Cycles of 19 and 2 years. Now, since in the former Chronology there are to the year 1817 exactly 140 Jubilees, or 20 cubes of 7, a period most perfect, it follows that there are in the Hebrew scheme, from the birth of Enos to 1818, exactly 140 — 26 = 114 Jubilees, or 294 Cycles, which, as uniting both the Metonic Cycle and the Jubilee, is also a perfect period. As, however, the series of *Jubilees* from the birth of Enos will again be brought into notice in treating of the Chronology of the Deluge, I forbear saying more of it here; but I shall, in the meanwhile, proceed to submit the Hebrew and Septuagint series of time from the birth of Enos to the test of the *Metonic Cycle.*

We have found that from the Hebrew era of his birth, B. C. 3769, to the year 1818, there is a period of 294, or 42 weeks of Cycles, and adding 1 Cycle we arrive at the year 1837. But on tracing down the series, according to the Chronology of Usher, I have not discovered that it touches any important eras in that Chronology, excepting the year B. C. 995, the 21st year of Solomon, when God appeared to him the second time, and, B. C. 976, being, according to Usher, the last year of that monarch, which, though not distinguished by any memorable event is, nevertheless, an era. The former year is from B.C. 3769 exactly 146 Cycles, but not a perfect period, and thence to 1818, are 148 Cycles. It hence follows, that the Hebrew date of the last year of Solomon exactly bisects the whole period, from the birth of Enos to the year 1818, in that Chronology; whereas, in the Greek, the bisecting point of the whole period of 6860 years, or 140 Jubilees, from the birth of Enos to the year 1817, is B.C. 1614, the 26th of the Exodus.*

Before I proceed to trace the great series of Cycles in the Septuagint, from the birth of Enos to the year 1816, I shall inform those readers who are unacquainted with my former Works, that there is also in that Chronology a series of Cycles terminating in the years 1818 and 1837. It begins in Adam's first year as a fallen creature, B.C. 5460. At the end of 48 Cycles it arrives at the 1st year of the administration of Seth, B.C. 4548. Thence, at the end of 70 Cycles, it touches the last year of the Antediluvian World, B.C. 3218. Thence 9 squares of 19 bring us to A.C. 32, the last year of our Lord's ministry. The series also touches many other great eras. Now, as the Hebrew series, from the birth of Enos, ending in 1818 and 1837, leads only to two insulated and unconnected dates, one of them being of secondary moment, the reader will at once see, from the details now given, that the Greek Chronology actually takes away from the Hebrew, as not appertaining to it, and, as its own legitimate property, takes exclusive possession of the series of Metonic Cycles leading to the years 1818 and 1837, demonstrating thereby the falsehood and corruption of the Hebrew series of Chronology.

I shall now show, in the following Table, what are the stupendous results which present themselves to our notice, in a series of Metonic Cycles computed from the birth of Enos, according to the Septuagint, B.C. 5044, and it may be safely affirmed, that such results could not possibly flow from any system of time concocted by the creature, and that they, therefore, bear upon them the stamp of uncreated wisdom.

* See my 'Fulness of the Times,' Table, page 173.

EVENTS.	DATES. Years B.C.	INTERVALS. Years.	Cycles of 19.	REMARKS.
The birth of Enos,	5044			
The birth of Shem,	3315	1729	91	Being 7 × 13, or 13 weeks of the Cycle of 19.
The death of Salah, and beginning of the administration of Eber,	2517	798	42	Being 7 × 6, or 6 weeks of the Cycle of 19. The whole period from the birth of Enos is 133 Cycles, being 19 weeks of Cycles = 7 squares of 19.
The birth of Jacob,	1985	532	28	Being 4 weeks of the Metonic Cycle, and from the birth of Shem 70 Cycles of 19 = 1330 years. From the birth of Enos 23 weeks of 19.
The last year of the administration of Gideon, the last of the Judges who appears to have had the visions of God,	1320	665	35	Being 5 weeks of 19, and the whole period from the birth of Enos is 28 × 7 = 196 *Cycles*, or 19 × 4 = 76 *Jubilees.*—It is absolutely perfect.
Sennacherib discomfited,	712	608	32	Or 8 × 4; and the whole period, from the birth of Enos, being 228 Cycles = 4332 years = 12 squares of 19.
	After Christ.			
Christ enters his 14th year, when under the law he was examinable, and subject to ordinances, and stood *in his own person,*	11	722	38	Being 2 squares of 19 years. This great era being properly that of the personal appearance of Messiah, is, from the birth of Enos, the square of 19 = 361 × 14 = 5054 years. From the birth of Shem it is 5 × 5 = 25 weeks of the Cycle of 19. From the accession of Eber it is 7 squares of 19. From the birth of Jacob, 15 weeks of 19. From the end of Gideon's administration it is 70 Cycles of 19. From the discomfiture of Sennacherib 2 squares of 19.
The first year of general peace after the terrible war of the French Revolution, being *the holding of the four winds of the Earth.* (Rev. vii. 1,)	1816	1805	95	Being 5 squares of 19, and from the birth of Enos the cube of 19 = 6859 years—from that of Shem, 270 Cycles of 19; from the birth of Jacob, 200 Cycles. For the relation of this era to that of the birth of Abraham, see Supplement to my Dissertation on the Seals, Preface, pp. iv, v. It is from his birth 27½ squares, and from his arrival at Haran, 27 squares of 12.

Events.	Dates. Years A.C.	Intervals. Years.	Cycles of 19.	Remarks.
The last change of administration in Great Britain, the great seat of the Church,	1835	19	1	The changes of administrations in the moral and intelligent universe, especially in those kingdoms which are connected with the Church, are only second in importance to the changes in the Church itself.—This era is from our Lord's 14th year 12 × 8 = 96 Cycles.

I observe, in the next place, that from the birth of Enos, B.C. 5044 to B.C. 4, which, in my former Works, has been proved to be the date of the conception of Christ, (who was born in Nisan, B. C. 3,) there is exactly the period of 1260 × 4 = 5040 years, being the square of 12 = 144 × 7 = 1008 × 5, or 35 squares of 12. Recalling to the recollection of the reader the circumstance, that we shall have occasion again to return to the *Jubilean* Chronology of the birth of Enos in connexion with that of the Deluge, I proceed now to try the Hebrew and Greek Chronologies of the period commencing at the birth of EBER.

We have seen that his birth is placed by the Septuagint in B.C. 2820, and the Hebrew B. C. 2281, the difference being 539 years, or 11 Jubilees exactly, and it results that a series of Jubilees from either date arrives at the same points of time in the ages posterior to the Hebrew date of his birth. It will accordingly be found, that from the former date, being that of the Septuagint, to the year 1836, are 95 Jubilees, or 245 Metonic Cycles, which, as uniting in itself 5 multiples of 19 Jubilees, or of 49 Cycles of 19, is a perfect period; and that from the latter or Hebrew date of the birth of Eber to 1836, there are 95 — 11 = 84 Jubilees, the multiple of 7 and 12, both perfect numbers, so that this period is also complete and perfect. Thus far the Hebrew date of the birth of Eber appears to rest on internal evidence equally strong with that of the Septuagint; but if we analyze both schemes, we shall immediately find that the Hebrew Series gives way.

In order to prove this, it will only be necessary to place in parallel columns the Greek and Hebrew Jubilean Series from the birth of Methuselah to the year B.C. 27, the epoch of the Augustan monarchy. The truth of the Greek, and spuriousness of the Hebrew, will be at once apparent to the discerning reader:

Events.	Dates. Years B.C. Greek.	Hebrew.	Intervals. Greek. Yrs.	Jubs.		Hebrew. Yrs.	Jubs.	Yrs.
The birth of Methuselah,	4192	3317						
The birth of Eber,	2820	2281	1372	28	These two periods are 4 + 2 = 6 cubes of 7.	1036	21	7
Abraham in his 12th year,	2134	1985	686	14		296	6	2
Isaac entreats for the barrenness of his wife. (Gen. xxv. 21,)	1987	1838	147	3		147	3	0
The last year of Jacob's bondage,	1889	1740	98	2	These three priods form the perfect one of 40 Jubilees.	98	2	0
Sennacherib invades Judah,	713	713	1176	24		1027	20	47
Octavianus receives the title of Augustus,	27	27	686	14		686	14	0
The whole period being in the Greek 85, or 17 × 5 Jubilees, is a complete number,			4165	85		3290	67	7

It will be seen, by reference to the Table at the end, that three of these *Hebrew dates* are also great eras in the *Greek Chronology*. The first, B.C. 3317, is that of the birth of Japhet; the third, B.C. 1985, is the Greek date of the birth, as the fourth, B.C. 1838, is of the death of Jacob. This is not the effect of *chance*, and it will be again noticed.

I shall next give the Greek series of Metonic Cycles from the birth of Eber, wherein will be found two of the foregoing Jubilean dates; but the era of Methuselah will not be found in it, as it belongs to another series of that Cycle:—

Events.	Dates. Years B.C.	Intervals. Years.	Cycles of 19.	Remarks.
The birth of Eber,	2820			
The last year of Jacob's Servitude,	1889	931	49	Or 19 Jubilees, and therefore a perfect period.
The 1st year of Cyrus in Persia,	559	1330	70	A perfect period, being 10 weeks of 19.

EVENTS.	DATES. Years B.C.	INTERVALS. Years.	Cycles of 19.	REMARKS.
Octavianus obtains the title of AUGUSTUS, the epoch of the AUGUSTAN MONARCHY,	27	532	28	Or 4 weeks of Cycles.
	After Christ.			
The English Liturgy published in Hebrew for the use of the Jews, and worship in the Hebrew tongue established in a congregation of believing Israelites for the first time in the annals of the Church of Christ,	1836	1862	98	Equal to the sum of the two preceding periods, being 14 weeks of the Cycle of 19, or 38 Jubilees; and from the birth of Eber, 245 Cycles, or 95 Jubilees.

Moreover, carrying up the Series, from the birth of Eber, B. C. 2820, to the penultimate year of the antediluvian world, when the ark was finished, B. C. 3219, we have 399 years = 21 Cycles, or 3 weeks of Cycles, which, added to the 49 Cycles that form the first period of the foregoing Series, make 70 Cycles. From the date last mentioned, B. C. 3219, ascending to the year of Adam's death, B. C. 4549, we have again 1330 years, or 70 Cycles. Thus, three periods of 70 Cycles are offered to us in this Series of time. 1st. From the death of Adam to the penultimate year of the antediluvian world;—2d. Thence to the last year of Jacob's Servitude;—and 3d. Thence to the 1st of Cyrus in Persia Proper. Lastly, as shown in my former Works, this Series ascends up to B. C. 5461, which, upon data that will be found in my Introductory Dissertation to the Fulness of the Times, I have endeavoured to fix as the year of the Fall of Adam. From that date to the birth of Eber are 2641 years, = 139 Cycles, viz., to the death of Adam, 48; to the penultimate year of the antediluvian world, 70; and to Eber, 21.

If, however, any of my readers think it proper to affirm that my date of the Fall, even granting the Septuagint Chronology to be true, does not rest on grounds which to them are satisfactory, I answer, that the remainder of the series, from the death of Adam downwards to 1836, does nevertheless contain internal evidence that its Author can be no other than the Creator, even if my date of the Fall be rejected. It is at any rate incumbent upon the advocates of the Hebrew Chronology to explain how any created intelligence could, by a happy chance, (since prescience is not attributable to the creature,) have laid down a series of generations and reigns containing these hitherto concealed and unknown harmonies of time. As well might it be said that the Epicurean hypothesis affords a right solution of the phenomena of the universe.

But I have not yet done with the great periods commencing from the birth of Eber, which, as he is in Gen. x. 21. distinguished after Shem as the father of the Hebrew race, is manifestly a great era.

From his birth, B. C. 2820, to the era of the French Revolution, 1789, are 4608 years, equal to the square of 12, or 144 multiplied by 32, or 4 × 8. This great period divides itself as follows:—

Events.	Dates. Years B.C.	Intervals. Years.	Squares of 12, &c.	Remarks.
The birth of Eber,	2820			
The departure of Jacob for Padan-aram,	1908	912	This period is not measured by the square of 12, but by 19 × 48.	These two periods are the square of 12 = 144 × 9 = 1296 years.
The 2d Servitude under Eglon,	1524	384	This period is 12 × 32.	
The second Temple finished,	516	1008	7 squares of 12	This date exactly bisects the whole period from the birth of Eber to the French Revolution of 1789.
	After Christ.			
The death of Odoacer, the end of the kingdom of the Heruli, and beginning of that of the Ostrogoths,	493	1008	7 squares of 12	This is a great era in history, and just 40 years before the invasion of Italy by Belisarius the general of Justinian.
Jerusalem taken by the Saracens,	637	144	1 square of 12	This date bisects the period from the finishing of the second Temple to 1789. It is from the birth of Eber 24 squares, and from the finishing of the second Temple 8 squares of 12.

EVENTS.	DATES. Years A.C.	INTERVALS. Years.	Squares of 12, &c.	REMARKS.
Charlemagne passes Easter at Rome. His second son, Pepin, is baptized by the Pope, who crowns him king of Italy,	781	144	1 square of 12	
The pacification of Lintz secures to the Protestants of Hungary the free exercise of their religion (Koch.)	1645	864	6 squares of 12	From the taking of Jerusalem by the Saracens 7 squares of 12.
The French Revolution,	1789	144	1 square of 12	From the birth of Eber 32 squares.

Computing next from the *Hebrew* date of the birth of Eber, B. C. 2281, a series of the square of 12, it arrives at the end of 28 squares at the year 1752, and 36 years more bring us to 1788, the date of the summoning of the States General of France; this, however, is not the end of a square of 12, but of the *fourth part* of the 29th square. On applying this series to history, I also have not found that its subdivisions do, as in the series from the Greek date of the birth of Eber, already placed before the reader, mark great eras. The bisection of this Hebrew series is, for example, B. C. 247, which is no era of the world or the church. But, bisecting the period from that year to 1788, it arrives at 771, which forms an exception to the foregoing remark, as it is the era of the reunion of the whole French monarchy under Charlemagne, after the death of his brother Carloman. I have discovered only two other periods of importance in this series; the one is B. C. 1705, being, according to Usher, the date of the sojourning of Israel in Goshen, at the end of 4 squares of 12 from B. C. 2281; the other is the date of Daniel's vision of the ram, B. C. 553, being the cube of 12 from the same year. But it is obvious that one or two insulated dates having no mutual connexion can afford no evidence of the authenticity of a period like this, since the ordinary chances of numbers will produce such results.

I shall observe, finally, that from the Greek date of the

birth of Eber, B. C. 2820, to the captivity of the Transjordanite tribes, B. C. 740, is the Cycle of 1040 × 2 = 2080 years, and thence to the calling of the States General of France are 133 Metonic Cycles, or 7 squares of 19 years. On the other hand, I have also just discovered that from the Hebrew date of the birth of Eber, B. C. 2281, to the finishing of the second Temple, B. C. 516, is the period of 1765 years, being the Cycle of 353 × 5; and at the end of it the moon is slow 5 H., 36 M., 3 S. Now, in order to account for this fact, consistently with the truth of the Septuagint date of the birth of Eber, let it be here observed that in that Chronology also, the *Hebrew date of his birth* is a *marked era*, being from the birth of Methuselah, B. C. 4192, exactly 39 Jubilees, and from the birth of Eber 11 Jubilees, and being itself the 14th year of Nahor the grandfather of Abraham. Moreover, carrying down from B. C. 2281, the prophetic period of 1260 years, it arrives at B. C. 1021, the year before the finishing of the first Temple; or carrying down the Cycle of 296 years (the Moon fast 5 H., 4 M. 52 S.,) it arrives at the birth of Jacob, B. C. 1985; or reckoning the Cycle of 372 years, (the Moon slow 3 H., 11 M., 30 S.,) it brings us to B. C. 1909, the year before Jacob's departure for Padan-aram; or computing by the Cycle of 353 years, then in the Greek Chronology 2 Cycles of 353 bring us to B. C. 1575, just 3 years before the first Servitude under Cushan-rishathaim, when the first apostasy of Israel was about consummated by the awful events recorded in Judges xviii—xxi. The third 353 years lead us to the sixth Servitude of 40 years under the Philistines, B. C. 1222, about the period of the birth of Samson. The fourth Cycle brings us to the accession of Jehoahaz of Israel on the death of Jehu, B. C. 869, and the fifth to the finishing of the second Temple, as already said. Now, as all the dates here referred to belong to the Greek and not the Hebrew scheme, excepting the last, which is common to both, it is hence quite apparent that the Septuagint Chronology appropriates to itself, and, as it were, takes possession of the *Hebrew date* of the birth of Eber as one of *its own periods*, having previously, by evidence the most triumphant, established its own date of his birth as the exact truth, and as one of the great epochs of universal history. Since writing the above, I have however discovered further unexpected evidence of the truth of the Greek era of Eber's birth, B. C. 2820. Reckoning from that year the Cycle and prophetical period of 2300 years, we arrive at the foundation of the second Temple in the 2d of Darius, B. C. 520, whence to the present year 1838, is the Cycle of 2357 years, the Moon fast 4 H., 32 M., 41 S. The whole from Eber to this year is 4657 years, a Cyclical period, being 334 × 13 = 4342 + 315; and at the end of it the Moon is fast 15 H., 17 M., 38 S., 53 TH.

Having thus, at different points of time, where the Greek and Hebrew Chronologies approach the nearest to an identity of Jubilean dates, analyzed both schemes, and shown that the former is marked with all those characters of exact science, which indicate that it is the contrivance of infinite wisdom, and that these characters are wholly wanting in the Hebrew, I shall now place before the reader certain other Chronological details leading to, and confirmatory of, the same conclusion.

One of the great questions at issue between the advocates of the Greek and Hebrew systems is with respect to the Postdiluvian Cainan, his very existence being denied by our Hebrew Chronologers, who therein flatly contradict the Evangelist Luke, and set aside his testimony.* It has already been shown by me, in the Preface to my Synopsis of Chronology, that the death of this patriarch is connected by great

* There is only one ancient copy of St Luke which omits Cainan, viz. the Cambridge MS., which our most learned men pronounce to be of little critical value. At any rate its testimony as to the genealogy of our Lord is worthless, for from the various readings in the 6th vol. of the London Polyglott, p. 11, which lies open before me, I see that the genealogy given by it in Luke iii. is altogether mutilated, being partly taken from St Matthew. As to this MS. see Horne, Vol. II. Part I. pp. 116, 117. I wish our Hebrew Chronology advocates, who are zealous for the credit of the unbelieving Jews, were a little more zealous for the honour of St Luke and the apostles of our Lord.

series of Metonic Cycles, with the deaths of Noah, Shem, and Arphaxad, with the births of Abraham and David, and the French Revolution in 1789, and also by a perfect Cycle with the year 1837.

I have, since that work was given to the public, discovered that from the death of the first Cainan, B. C. 3944, to the birth of the second or Postdiluvian Cainan, B. C. 3080, are exactly 6 squares of 12 = 864 years; and that the whole series from the former date to the year 1817, when the New Testament was given to the Jews in Hebrew, comprehends exactly 40 squares of 12, or 5760 years divided as follows:—

Events.	Dates. Years B. C.	Intervals. Years.	Squares of 12.	Remarks.
The *first* Cainan dies,	3944			
The *second* Cainan born,	3080	864	6	These 2 periods are 1 cube of 12.
The year before the birth of Terah, and probably that of his conception,	2216	864	6	
Joseph dies,	1784	432	3	Or one-fourth of the cube of 12.
God appears to Moses at Horeb,	1640	144	1	Being 16 squares from the death of the first Cainan.
The 7th year of the reign of David, being the year before he reigned in Jerusalem,	1064	576	4	This date bisects the whole period from the death of the 1st Cainan to 1817.
	After Christ.			
The second year of the 1st Crusade,	1097	2160	15	This era is from the death of the first Cainan, 7 × 5 = 35 squares of 12, or 1260 × 4 = 5040 years.
The Lutherans assume the name of PROTESTANTS,	1529	432	3	This date is from the same event, 19 × 2 = 38 squares of 12, or 288 Metonic Cycles.
The New Testament published in Hebrew for the Jews. Also the evacuation of France by the allies begun, and one-fifth of the army of occupation withdrawn,	1817	288	2	From the death of the *first* Cainan, 40 squares; and from the birth of the *second* Cainan, 17 × 2 = 34 squares.

Applying the test of the square of 12 to the Hebrew date

of the death of the first Cainan, B. C. 2769, I find a perfect period of 32 squares comes out in the year 1840, which is shown in my Works to be a great era. When, however, this series is analyzed and applied to the Hebrew Chronology, I do not discover that it touches any important eras, or that it is distinguished by any characters of similarity to the above stupendous series in the Greek Chronology. It carries on no connected chain of events.

I shall, in concluding this part of my subject, briefly mention some other periods.

There is from the birth of Jared in the Greek Chronology, B. C. 4519, a series of 44 squares of 12 to the year 1818. It is as follows:—

EVENTS.	DATES. Years B. C.	INTERVALS. Years.	Squares of 12.	REMARKS.
The birth of Jared,	4519			
The 1st year of the administration of Mahalaleel, being the year after the death of the 1st Cainan,	3943	576	4	
The birth of Terah,	2215	1728	12	The cube of 12.
The year before the call of Abraham,	2071	144	1	
The Exodus,	1639	432	3	This great era is, from the birth of Jared, 20 squares.
David's 1st year in Jerusalem,	1063	576	4	This great era is 2 cubes of 12 from the birth of Jared.
	After Christ.			
The 3d year of the 1st Crusade,	1098	2160	15	This era is, from the Exodus, 19 squares, or 144 Metonic Cycles.
The Confession of Augsburg and Smalcaldic league,	1530	432	3	This great era is 42 = 7 × 6, that is, 6 weeks of the square of 12 from the birth Jared.
The Congress of Aix la Chapelle, and final evacuation of France,	1818	288	2	The whole from the birth of Jared is 11 × 4 = 44 squares of 12, a most complete period.

Again, from the death of Enos, B. C. 4139, to the Dedication of the first Temple, B. C. 1019, is precisely the Cycle of 1040 × 3 = 3120 years, and the reader will recollect that from Creation to the same era are 91 Jubilees, or 13 Cubes of 7. Next, from the Dedication, B. C. 1019, to the present year, 1838, are 12 × 7 = 84 × 34 = 2856 years, which is a complete period, being two sacred numbers multiplied into each other, and both by 17 × 2 = 34; and the whole period, from the death of Enos, is the square of 12 × 41½.

Let me also here point out the following deep analogy: From the death of Lamech, B. C. 3252, to the Deluge, B. C. 3217, when the FOUNTAINS OF THE GREAT DEEP of the NATURAL EARTH were broken up, there are 35 YEARS; and from the death of Lamech, to the French Revolution of 1789, which was the beginning of the breaking up of the FOUNTAINS OF THE GREAT DEEP of the MORAL AND POLITICAL WORLD, are 35 SQUARES of 12. The number 35, or 7 × 5, is the measure of both periods,—the one being *years*, the other *squares of twelve years*.

I shall finally mention that, from the death of Methuselah, B. C. 3223, to B. C. 1143, the date of the death of Eli, and the termination of St Paul's period of 450 years (Acts xiii. 20.), are exactly 2 Cycles of 1040, and thence to 1798, the second act of the great war of the French Revolution, when, after the short pause of the peace of Campo Formio, it broke out again with new fury, are 60 Jubilees, or 12 × 5.

SECTION II.

It is among the axioms in mathematics, that subtracting equal quantities from equal, or adding them to equal, the remainders or the sums are equal. In astronomical science it is not equally an axiom, that subtracting Cycles from Cycles the remainders, or adding them, the sums are Cycles; for it has been shown by me that the Metonic Cycle, multiplied beyond a certain number, produces sums of years that are not Cycles.* Still, however, it must be observed, that there are certain Cyclical characters even in such sums, for they are the exact multiples of the original Cycle of 19, and being further multiplied they again produce Cycles which recur in perpetual circles, being still exact multiples of the original root 19. It therefore holds generally, though not universally true, that from Cycles subtracting periods which are Cyclical, or adding them, the remainders or the sums are Cycles, either more perfect or less perfect than the originals, according to the circumstances of each particular case. How this principle is to be made subservient to the elucidation of the subject we are discoursing upon, will now be explained.

It is shown in my Synopsis of Chronology, that, from B. C. 3219, the penultimate year of the Antediluvian World, when the Ark was finished, also from the year of the Flood, B. C. 3217, and the year of the birth of Arphaxad, B. C. 3215, there are great series of Cycles coming out in our own times.

* Synopsis of Chronology, p. 10.

Next, by the Table at the end, it will be seen that the exact difference between the Greek and Hebrew Chronologies, at each of the foregoing eras, is 869 years, which is an imperfect Cycle, consisting of the following:

	D.	H.	M.	S.	TH.
315 × 2 = 630, the Moon fast		6	1	33	4
11 years, ——	1	12	6	15	52
641 —— ——	1	18	7	48	56
19 × 12 = 228 years, Moon slow	1	0	49	7	
At the end of 869 years Moon fast	0	17	18	41	56

Now, since there are in the Septuagint Chronology, from the finishing of the Ark, B. C. 3219, to the fall of the French Monarchy, in 1792, exactly 5010 years, which is the Cycle of 334 years multiplied by 15, at the end of which the Moon is *fast* 14 H. 10 M. 14 S. 15 TH.: and it being now shown that at the end of 869 years (the amount of the difference between the two Chronologies, at this era of the finishing of the Ark), the Moon is *fast* more than 17 hours, as above, it follows that at the end of 5010 — 869 = 4141 years, she is *slow* the amount of the difference between 17 H. 18 M. 41S. 56 TH. and 14 H. 10 M. 14 S. 15 TH.; that is, 3 H. 8 M. 27 S. 41 TH.

From the Hebrew date of the finishing of the Ark, B. C. 2350, to the year 1792, there is thus a cyclical period of 4141 years, which consists of the Cycle of 1040 years × 3 = 3120 and that of 1021, for the errors of which Cycles I refer to my Synopsis,* and at the end of it the Moon is little more than 3 hours behind the Sun, whereas the error of the Cycle, which measures the same period in the Greek Chronology, is more than 14 hours. In like manner the Cycle from the Hebrew Diluvian era, B. C. 2348, to the year 1813, the date of the second overthrow of Napoleon, being exactly that of 1040 × 4 = 4160, at the end of which the Moon is slow

* It may be proper here to inform the reader that the word *error* is not here used in its common, but in an astronomical, sense. It signifies the amount of time which the Sun and Moon have deviated from each other, at the end of a Cycle, supposing they were in conjunction at the beginning of it, or from their relative positions in the heavens at the beginning of it.

5 H. 12 M. 33 S. 16 TH. is more perfect than the period of 5029 years, which measures the same interval in the Greek, the Moon being fast at the end of this period 12 H. 6 M. 8 S. 40 TH.

I shall meet the argument, which may be raised from these results, in favour of the Hebrew Chronology, by remarking that where there are scientific numbers of like character, measuring the same great periods of Mundane History in both Chronologies, it is manifest that the mere fact of the existence of these numbers cannot be conclusive in favour of either Chronology, since they are found in both.—As the only means of discovering the truth, it becomes necessary, in such cases, to analyze the different parts, and to submit both schemes, the Greek and Hebrew, where these Cyclical harmonies meet, to *other tests.* I shall, therefore, place before the reader a comparative analysis of the foregoing Cyclical periods in both Chronologies:—

EVENTS.	DATES. YEARS B. C.		INTERVALS. YEARS.		CHARACTERS OF THE PERIODS WHICH MEASURE THE INTERVALS.	
	Greek.	Hebrew.	Greek.	Hebrew.	Greek.	Hebrew.
The penultimate year of the Antediluvian period when the Ark was finished,	3219	2350				
Joseph exalted in Egypt,	1864	1715	1355	635	A perfect Cycle, Moon fast 1 H. 42 M. 38 S.	Not Cyclical at all.
The 13th year of Darius Hystaspes, when he sent an expedition to India, and the beginning of Daniel's 2300 years,	509	509	1355	1206	Do. Do.	Not Cyclical at all, but the two periods 635 + 1206 = 1841 years, are an imperfect Cycle 1040 + 687 + 19 × 6, the Moon being slow at the end of it 13 H. 53 M. 25 S. 30 TH.
	After Christ.					
The fall of the French monarchy, and beginning of the great war of the Revolution,	1792	1792	2300	2300	A Cycle, the Moon fast 10 H. 44 M. 57 S. 49 TH.	
	Total,		5010	4141	The Cycle of (334 × 5 = 1670) × 3.	The Cycle of 1040 × 3 = 3120 + 1021.

Now, as to its arithmetical properties, the number of 5010 years is much more perfect than the Hebrew number of 4141, the former having for its basis the perfect Cycle of 334 years, multiplied by 5 and 3, both of which are sacred numbers, and the latter, not reducible to parts without a remainder, being a prime.—I shall, however, observe, that it is Daniel's period of 2300 years which affords us the means of certainly establishing the genuineness of the foregoing Greek, and the consequent falsehood of the Hebrew Series; since, were it not for that period, the series being divided as follows, would show results much more favourable to the Hebrew :—

The Hebrew date of the finishing of the Ark is B. C. 2350; reckoning thence the Cycle of 1355 years, which is the measure of the two first intervals in the Greek Series, we arrive at the Hebrew date of Solomon's 21st year,* when God appeared to him the second time, B. C. 995. 1 Kings ix. 1, 10.

Now, were we to leave out the 2300 years, and reckon from the last date to the year 1792, we should have, as the intervening period, B. C. 995 + A. C. 1792 = 2786 years, which is a Cycle, at the end of which the Moon is slow only 4 H. 51 M. 5 S. 54 TH. But, on the other hand, computing from B. C. 995 to the beginning of Daniel's 2300 years, the interval is 486 years, a very imperfect Cycle, composed of 353 + 19 × 7 = 133, at the end of which the Moon is slow 15 H. 36 M. 3 S. 43 TH.; and thence to 1792 we have the Cycle of 2300, the Moon fast, as above mentioned, more than 10 hours. It is evident, therefore, that, leaving out the 2300 years, the Hebrew series becomes more perfect than the Greek; but since that number is a great Scriptural period, forming an essential part of the series of Cycles from the finishing of the Ark to the year 1792, it cannot be omitted, for on it hangs the prophetic arrangement of the times of the World. This number, therefore, as already said, enables us certainly to show the spuriousness of the Hebrew Chronology

* In the Greek, Solomon's 21st year does not come into this Series, but into that from the birth of Arphaxad.

of this period, as it utterly destroys the Cyclical harmony of the foregoing Hebrew series, leaving the Greek whole and entire with all the evidence of the divine skill and workmanship, which is the result of the perfect harmony of all its parts. It might also, at any rate, have been justly maintained, that the second appearance of God to Solomon is not an event sufficient to prove the truth of any series of Chronology, unless it were connected with other similar eras by scientific periods. It has no discoverable relation to the other events of the foregoing Hebrew series, of which it forms one of the disjointed links. But it will be seen below, that in the Greek Chronology it is connected by scientific time with God's appearance to Moses.

Were any further argument necessary, after what has now been said, to establish the truth of the Greek Chronology from the era of the finishing of the Ark, it would be found in the stupendous Series, from the Fall, B. C. 5461, or, (if any readers do not think that date sufficiently proved,*) from the death of Adam, B. C. 4549, the birth of Eber, B. C. 2820, and other great eras, to the year 1836; for of this Series, the year B. C. 3219, that of the finishing of the Ark, is an essential part, being, as we have seen before,† 70 Cycles from the death of Adam, and 140 before the 1st of Cyrus in Persia Proper. Also, from B. C. 3219, is the perfect period, to 1836, of 14 squares of 19; and from the same date to 1822, the termination of Daniel's period of 1290 years, is the prophetical period of 1260 years multiplied by 4, or 35 squares of 12 = 5040 years.

I shall now give an analysis of the Cyclical periods in both Chronologies from the Deluge to the year 1813, and from the birth of Arphaxad to the year 1826.

* See, with respect to this date, the Introductory Dissertation to the Fulness of the Times, Section I.

† Page 21.

Events.	Dates. Years B.C. Greek.	Hebrew.	Intervals. Greek.	Hebrew.	Characters of the Periods which measure the Intervals. Greek.	Hebrew.
The Deluge,	3217	2348				
	After Christ.					
The final overthrow of the Gothic kingdom in Italy, a great era of universal history and prophecy,	553	553	3769	2900	A perfect Cycle; the Moon only 3 M., 2 S., fast.	A period very imperfectly Cyclical, consisting of 2080 + 687 + 19 × 7; the Moon at the end of it slow 17 H., 15 M., 39 S., 24 TH.
The second great overthrow of Napoleon at Leipsick,	1813	1813	1260	1260	A Cycle; the Moon fast 12 H., 3 M., 6 S.	

SERIES FROM THE BIRTH OF ARPHAXAD.

Events.	Years B.C. Greek.	Hebrew.	Intervals. Greek.	Hebrew.	Greek.	Hebrew.
The birth of Arphaxad,	3215	2346				
God appears to Moses at the Bush,	1640	1491	1575	855	The Cycle of 315 × 5.	45 Cycles of 19.
The second appearance of God to Solomon in the 21st of his reign,	1010	995	630	496	The Cycle of 315 × 2, and from the birth of Arphaxad 1 week of that Cycle.	The period is not Cyclical at all.
The end of the Greek kingdom of Syria, when the Romans appeared as the *fourth* kingdom of Daniel, on the theatre of scriptural action,	65	65	945	930	The Cycle of 315 × 3, and the whole period, from the birth of Arphaxad, 10 Cycles.	The period is not Cyclical at all; but the 3 periods, 855 + 496 + 930 = 2281 years, are a Cycle, composed of 2080 + 19 × 10 = 190 + 11; at the end of which the Moon is fast 12 H., 49 M., 3 S., 24 TH.
	After Christ.					
The meeting of the last Protestant Parliament of Great Britain,	1826	1826	1890	1890	The Cycle of 315 × 6; the Moon fast 18 H., 4 M., 39 S., 12 TH.	
The whole period is			5040	4171		

It will be manifest to the attentive reader, that in both these Series, the intermediate links in the chain of Cyclical time, are either altogether wanting, or are imperfect in the Hebrew. In either Series the evidence of superintending omniscience and power is seen in the Greek Chronology, which bears on it the marks of originality; for certainly that which is most perfect and most exact must be the original, and that which is less perfect in its subdivisions must be spurious and forged. It also demands notice, that the number of 5040 years, which is the measure of the last Series, is one of a very peculiar character. It is, as already said, the prophetical period of 1260 years multiplied by 4. Now, it is shown by Chesaux, that this number is most perfect, resolving itself into no less than 35 different factors; and here we have it quadrupled, the sum being itself the square of 12, the number of the sanctuary multiplied by 35, and either 720 WEEKS of years, or 420 TWELVES. In all respects, then, this is a number of mysterious FULNESS, and a fit measure of the great periods of the Almighty. Moreover, this Series, of which it is the whole length, includes some of the greatest epochs of the Divine ages:—1st. The birth of the first man after the Flood;—2d. The beginning of the dispensation of Moses;—3d. The acme of that dispensation;—4th. The appearance and first dominion of the Romans, as the fourth kingdom of Daniel, on the theatre of scriptural action;—5th. The first of the Septenary of years from 1826 to 1833, wherein those mighty events took place in the East and West, which have wholly changed the political position of the nations occupying the territories of the four kingdoms of Daniel, and are, as is evident to all intelligent persons, only preparing the way for other and more stupendous events yet in the womb of time.

The number of 4171 years, which in the Hebrew Chronology measures the foregoing period, possesses none of these arithmetical properties, not being divisible by 2, 3, 4, 5, 6, or 7, but I think a prime.

I next proceed, in connexion with the Chronology of the period of the Deluge, to investigate, as was proposed in a former page, the Jubilean Chronology, both Greek and Hebrew, of the era of the birth of Enos; and the reason of my deferring it till now will be apparent from the following Series, beginning at the Hebrew date of his birth, wherein it will be seen that the Scribes have included the Deluge as one main link of the chain of Jubilean time. This Series is, I think, the MASTERPIECE of the framers of that Chronology, bearing upon it such marks of *deep contrivance*, that, were it not quite apparent in what manner it was effected, it would be almost impossible to believe it a forgery, and not to receive it as the exact truth.

EVENTS.	DATES IN THE HEBREW CHRONOLOGY.	INTERVALS.		REMARKS.
	Years B.C.	Years.	Jubilees.	
The birth of Enos,	3769			
The birth of Shem,	2446	1323	27	27 is the cube of 3, and is one of the numbers of frequent occurrence in the Sacred Chronology.
The Flood,	2348	98	2	This is the true interval from the birth of Shem to the Flood.
Jacob goes to Padan-aram,	1760	588	12	A perfect period; and from the birth of Shem to this great era, 14 Jubilees, or 2 cubes of 7.
The first foundation of the SECOND TEMPLE, Ezra iii. 8,	535	1225	25	The square of 5, and a complete period.
	After Christ.			
Christ 8 years, according to Usher's date of the Nativity, B. C. 4, but only 7 years complete according to the true date of his birth, B. C. 3,	5	539	11	From the birth of Enos, the whole period is 77 Jubilees, or 11 × 7, or the Cycle of 1078 years × 3½. From the birth of Shem, 50 Jubilees; from the Deluge, 48,—all perfect numbers.
The Congress of Aix-la-Chapelle, and the final evacuation of France.	1818	1813	37	The whole period is 114 Jubilees, or 294 Metonic Cycles; and it is perfect, as uniting both these measures of time, but it is not divisible by 7 or 12.
The whole period is,		5586	114	
The end of Daniel's 1335 years,	1867	49	1	
		5635	115	

It is unnecessary to inform the reader, that the advocates of the Hebrew Chronology must, to be consistent, maintain this Series to be the *original*, and the *exact truth*. I now proceed to show, that it is *spurious* and *corrupt*; and I request the patient and close attention of the reader, to the evidence I shall place before him.

In the Greek Chronology the birth of Enos is placed in B. C. 5044, that of Enoch B. C. 4357, which is the Cycle of 687 years, or 14 Jubilees and 1 year from the former era; and the Deluge is placed in B. C. 3217, being, from the birth of Enos, 37 Jubilees and 14 years = 1827.

From these three dates, computing series of Jubilees, there are, from the birth of Enos to the year A. C. 1817, 140 Jubilees, or 20 Septenaries of the Jubilee, and to 1866, a Jubilee more = 141. From the birth of Enoch there are, to 1818, exactly 126 Jubilees, or 7 × 18; and to 1867, one Jubilee = 127. From the Deluge there are, to the year 1831, when the Egyptian army entered Palestine, and the Reform Bill was brought in, exactly 103 Jubilees; or, if we reckon the Series from the birth of Shem, 2 Jubilees higher, it is 105, or 15 Septenaries of the Jubilee, to the year 1831.

I shall next give a Table of each of these Series of Jubilees:—

GREEK SERIES FROM THE BIRTH OF ENOS.

EVENTS.	DATES. Years B.C.	INTERVALS. Years.	Jubilees.	REMARKS.
The birth of Enos,	5044			
The conception of Enoch,	4358	686	14	These three periods are each perfect, and being added, are 8 × 8 = 64 Jubilees,—a complete period.
The confusion of tongues, and beginning of the division of the earth,	2398	1960	40	
Jacob goes to Padan-aram,	1908	490	10	
The proclamation of Cyrus, and end of the captivity,	536	1372	28	4 weeks of Jubilees, or cubes of 7; and from the division of the earth, 38 Jubilees, or 98 Metonic Cycles, a perfect period.

Events.	Dates. After Christ.	Intervals. Years.	Jubilees.	Remarks.
The 7th year of our Lord's age,	4	539	11	From the division of the earth 49 Jubilees, or 7 cubes of 7.
The New Testament in Biblical Hebrew given to the Jews,	1817	1813	37	
Total from the birth of Enos,		6860	140	Or 20 Cubes of 7.
The last of Daniel's 1335 years,	1866	49	1	
Total to 1866,		6909	141	

GREEK SERIES FROM THE BIRTH OF ENOCH

	Before Christ.			
The birth of Enoch,	4357			
The birth of Reuben,	1907	2450	50	These 2 periods are 57 Jubilees, or 147 Cycles, and uniting in themselves those measures of time, they form a perfect period.
The beginning of the administration of Othniel, the first of the judges,	1564	343	7	
Ditto Abimelech,	1319	245	5	The administration of Abimelech is an era; for Gideon, whom he succeeded, was the last of the judges, except Samson, who received his commission immediately from the Lord. Samson was about 96 years later. From Reuben to this date, are 12 Jubilees.
The 3d year of the building of the Temple,	1025	294	6	From Enoch are 17 × 4 = 68 Jubilees, and from Reuben to this era are 18 Jubilees, being the 7th part of the whole period, from the birth of Enoch to the year 1818.
The foundation of the second Temple in the 2d of Cyrus. Ezra iii. 8—18.	535	490	10	Being from the beginning of the Administration of Othniel, 21 Jubilees, or 3 Cubes of 7, and from that of Abimelech, 16 Jubilees, or 4 × 4.
	After Christ.			
Christ 7 years complete; the end of the 66th week of Daniel's 70 weeks,	5	539	11	Being, from the birth of Enoch, 89 Jubilees, and from the administration of Othniel 32, and from the 3d year of the building of the Temple, 21 Jubilees, or 3 Cubes of 7.

Events.	Dates. After Christ.	Intervals. Years.	Jubilees.	Remarks.
The Congress of Aix-la-Chapelle, and the final evacuation of France,	1818	1813	37	
Total from the birth of Enoch,		6174	126	Or 18 Cubes of 7.
The termination of Daniel's period of 1335 years,	1867	49	1	I shall here mention that from the era of Creation, B. C. 5478, to 1867, there are exactly 51 squares of 12 = 7344 years, being 4¼ Cubes of 12.
Total, to 1867,		6223	127	

GREEK SERIES FROM THE BIRTH OF SHEM.

	Years B.C.			
Shem born,	3315			
The Flood,	3217	98	2	These three periods make the sum of 9 × 5 = 45 Jubilees.
The birth of Joseph,	1894	1323	27	
The accession of Saul,	1110	784	16	
	After Christ.			
Our Lord in his 21st year,	18	1127	23	From Shem to our Lord's 21st year, are 17 × 4 = 68 Jubilees, and from the Flood 66 Jubilees, or the Cycle of 1078 × 3 = 3234 years.
Vespasian enters Galilee with 60,000 men,	67	49	1	From the accession of Saul, to the entrance of the Roman army, are 12 × 2 = 24 Jubilees.
Rome besieged by Astolphus and the Lombards. Pope Stephen goes into France for succour, and declares Pepin and his sons patricians of Rome, but stipulates for the cession of the Exarchate of Ravenna, which took place in 756,	753	686	14	From the fall of Jerusalem by the Roman sword in 70 to 756, when the Exarchate was ceded to the Papacy, which was the beginning of its temporal power, there are also exactly 14 Jubilees, or 2 cubes of 7.
The armies of the first Crusade march for the East,	1096	343	7	From our Lord's 21st year to the Crusades are 22 Jubilees, or the Cycle of 1078 years. The Crusades are from the Deluge that Cycle × 4 = 4312 years.
England acknowledges the independence of the United States,	1782	686	14	
The entrance of the Egyptian army into Palestine, and the Reform Bill brought in,	1831	49	1	Erom the accession of Saul to the entrance of the Egyptian army are 12 × 5 = 60 Jubilees.
Total from the birth of Shem,		5145	105	Or 15 cubes of 7.

I shall now point out the mode in which the Rabbis have, from the *first* and *third* of these series, formed their own Jubilean series from the birth of Enos to the foundation of the second Temple, B. C. 535. As they have curtailed the whole Chronology from Enos to the Christian era, just 1 year more than 26 Jubilees,* the effect of this is to throw the Jubilean series from the birth of Enos 1 year later, and to make each Jubilee come out in the very years which, in the Greek Chronology, fall out as Jubilees,—not, be it observed, in the series from the birth of *Enos*, but in that from the birth of *Enoch;* or, to express this in fewer words, they have, in the spurious Chronology, identified their own series from the birth of Enos, with that of the Septuagint, from the birth of Enoch. In the next place, there being, in the Greek Chronology, from Enos to the Deluge, 1827 years, which is 14 years more than 37 Jubilees, the Jewish Scribes, in curtailing this interval, have contrived that the whole sum of years subtracted should also be 14 years more than 8 Jubilees, the effect of which is to bring the dates of the birth of Shem and the Deluge also into the Series of Jubilees, computed from the birth of Enos, so that the *first* and *third* of the foregoing Greek Series are blended into one. The truth of this will appear evident by a simple process of subtraction:—

The Greek interval from the birth of Enos, B.C.	5044		
To the Deluge, ...	3217		
Is 1827 years, or	37 Jubilees,	14 years.	
Subtract	8	14	
The remainder is the present Hebrew Chronology of this period, whereby the birth of Shem and the Deluge are brought into the Jubilean Series, from Enos, ...	29 Jubilees,	0 years.	

The amount of 100 years struck off from each of the 4 generations of Enos, Cainan, Mahalaleel, and Enoch, and 6 from that of Lamech, is exactly 406 years, or 8 Jubilees and

* See Table at the end.

14 years. By these deep artifices, it must be confessed that the Rabbis have formed a Series, which, on a first superficial view, appears, as already said, stamped with all the characters of originality and truth; nor can it be gainsaid that they have done it with consummate ability.

As, however, they have not brought the birth of Enoch into this Series, it becomes necessary to apply to the era of that patriarch, in the Hebrew Chronology, the test of the Jubilee, seeing that in the Greek a great Series from his birth, to the year 1818, has been laid before the reader. The birth of Enoch in the Hebrew is B. C. 3382, from which a period of 106 Jubilees comes out in 1813; but that number, not being divisible by 3, 4, 5, 12, or 7, is altogether imperfect. Moreover, the only eras in the Hebrew Chronology which the Series touches, are, 1st, the death of Lamech, B. C. 2353, which is from the above Hebrew date of the birth of Enoch, 21 Jubilees, or 1029 years;—2d. at the end of 1764 years, or 36 Jubilees more, it arrives at the second year of the siege of Jerusalem by Nebuchadnezzar, B. C. 589, and these two periods being added, are exactly equal to the first two in the *Greek Jubilean Series* from the birth of Enoch, which is another evidence of the deep subtlety of the corrupters of the Chronology;—3d. and lastly, from B. C. 589 to B. C. 1, the date of the return of Joseph and Mary with the infant Jesus from Egypt, are 12 Jubilees, and thence to 1813 are 37; but as the Chronology of these two periods is common to both the Greek and Hebrew schemes, no argument in favour of either can be grounded upon it.

I shall now, however, state, that the *Hebrew date* of the *death of Lamech* is also, in the *Greek Chronology*, a conspicuous era. It is just 6 years before the death of Peleg, when he was 333 years complete, at which time the division of the earth, if not already finished, must have been about finishing, for Peleg was born in B. C. 2686, which, minus 333, gives, B. C. 2353, the Hebrew date of the death of Lamech. Reckoning then a series of Jubilees, according to the Greek Chronology, from that date, it is as follows:—

Events.	Dates B.C.	Intervals. Years.	Jubilees.	Remarks.
Peleg 333 years old, and the division of the earth, which was begun 45 years before, about completed,	2353			In the Hebrew Chronology this is the date of the death of Lamech.
Ishmael born,	2059	294	6	In the Hebrew Chronology the birth of Ishmael being, B.C. 1910, is, from their date of the death of Lamech, 9 Jubilees and 2 years.
The 1st year of plenty in Egypt, and 2d of Joseph's administration,	1863	196		
The accession of Solomon,	1030	833	17	Being 21 Jubilees from the birth of Ishmael, or 3 cubes of 7.
The 2d year of the siege of Jerusalem,	589	441	9	Being from the birth of Ishmael 30 Jubilees,—a complete period.
The return of Joseph and Mary with the child Jesus from Egypt,	1	588	12	Being from the division 48 Jubilees; from the birth of Ishmael 42, or 6 cubes of 7; and from the accession of Solomon 21 Jubilees, or 3 cubes.
	After Christ.			
The overthrow of Napoleon at Leipsick,	1813	1813	37	The whole period, from the 333d year complete of Peleg, is 85 Jubilees, or 17 × 5.

In this series, according to the Greek Chronology, there are thus *four great eras* between the age of Peleg and the return of the holy family from Egypt, whereas in the Hebrew series we have only *one.* It is therefore manifest, that the Jubilean evidence does here wholly preponderate against the Hebrew and in favour of the Greek Chronology. We have, in the first place, in this Chronology, a perfect series of 18 cubes of 7, or 126 Jubilees from the birth of Enoch to the year 1818, while that from the Hebrew date of his birth to 1813, is altogether imperfect in its sum total, and also presents to us the Chronological paradox that, from the date of the death of Lamech to the siege of Jerusalem by Nebuchadnezzar, there is no intermediate marked Jubilean era. 2dly. The Greek Chronology, by offering to us a better and more complete Jubilean series than the Hebrew, for the whole period from B. C. 2353, the Hebrew era of the death of Lamech, to the year 1813, does in effect take possession of it as its own, and drives the Hebrew from it.

I must also refer the reader to the series of Metonic Cycles from Creation to the year 1838, for further irrefragable evidence of the truth of the Septuagint date of the birth of Enoch, it being there shown, that it is connected with the Deluge and the death of Christ, as well as other great eras, by perfect series of that Cycle.* Moreover, as the date of his translation is closely connected with that of his birth, and results from it, I shall here state, that from the last year of his preaching, or the year before his translation, being in the Greek Chronology, B. C. 3993, to the birth of Joseph, B. C. 1894, is the Cycle of 2099 years, the Moon being slow 4 H., 40 M., 22 S., 13 TH., at the end of it; and thence to the present year, 1838, are 3731 years, which is also a Cycle equal to that of $334 \times 10 = 3340 + 391$, and at the end of it the Moon is fast 4 H., 11 M., 13 S., 42 TH. The whole period from the year before the translation of Enoch to 1838, is the perfect Cycle of 5830 years, the Moon at the end of it being slow 29 M., 8 S., 31 TH.

Let it now be distinctly kept in view, what it is which the advocates of the Hebrew Chronology ask of us, with reference to the Chronology of the periods from the birth of Enos and Enoch and Shem. We are required by them to believe, that out of their own two Jubilean series, one of which, from the birth of Enos, being 114 Jubilees, or 294 Metonic Cycles, and therefore uniting in itself these two great measures of time, is perfect, but not being a cube of 7, or a multiple of 12, or 5 or 10, does not possess the perfection of any of these numbers; and the other of which, from the birth of Enoch, and consisting of 106 Jubilees, is absolutely imperfect

* See p. 11.

in its sum total, and more so in its subdivisions.—We are required, we say, to believe that out of these two series, the authors of the Septuagint Chronology have, by forged and fraudulent additions to the generations of the patriarchs, and the administrations and reigns of judges and kings, constructed three different series, one of 140 Jubilees, or 20 cubes of 7, the second of 126 Jubilees, or 18 cubes, and the third of 105 Jubilees, or 15 cubes of that number, that is, each of them being perfect multiples, of the cube, of the very number of perfection, besides a fourth series, of which the sum total is $17 \times 5 = 85$, and therefore, though less perfect than the former, yet a complete number. But further, these series are not perfect only in their sums total. It will be found that each series contains in itself, by the entire harmony and proportions of its subdivisions, evidences of its truth, which are absolutely inimitable, being stamped with the characters of perfection and power, which belong to the arrangements of HIM, who ordained the ages of the intelligent universe, and without whom not a sparrow falleth to the ground. The advocates of the Hebrew scheme, do thus in effect require us to believe, that which is *most perfect* in complex harmony, to be *corrupt*, and that which is *less perfect*, to be *incorrupt* and *true;* and that the *Greek forgers*, as they allege them to be, have given to their fabric, evidences of variegated harmony and order, which do not appertain to that Chronology, viz. the Hebrew, which *they* affirm to be the work of the Creator himself. They thus require us to break down and annihilate all the principles of moral evidence, in order that we may arrive at the conclusion, and set our seal to its truth, that the unbelieving Jews of the three first centuries, from whom was received by the Church, the Hebrew text which is now extant, were more worthy of credit than the apostles and their successors, with the whole primitive Church, since they acknowledged the Septuagint text, wherein we have the longer Chronology, to be a faithful version, and accordingly adopted its computation. Moreover, all this is required of us for no better reason, as it appears to me, than that it would be wrong to suspect the crucifiers and blasphemers of the Lord of glory, and the bitterest enemies in that age, and persecutors of his Church, of having corrupted the Hebrew text in the generations of the patriarchs,* in which is evidently included the dilemma, either that the apostles and apostolic church, did connive at that in the Greek text, which the Hebrew doctors are supposed incapable to have effected in the Hebrew, or that they were imposed upon, and remained ignorant of the existence of the fraud. Moreover, that which raises this argument, as it were, to the climax of absurdity, is the fact which we have before our eyes, that the Jews have undeniably proved themselves the most arrant forgers, having, in their popular and received system of Chronology, that of Ganz, still further shortened the Chronology by no less a period than 244 years, their mundane era being B. C. 3760, while that which Usher draws from the Hebrew text is B. C. 4004.

It was not till I was far advanced in the composition of these pages that I perceived that Usher's era of Creation, B. C. 4004, is precisely the amount of the Cycle of 1040 years lower down in the Chronology than the Greek era of the birth of Enos, B. C. 5044. It consequently falls into the series of Cycles proved, in my Synopsis of Chronology, to run from the birth of Enos to the French Revolution in 1789.† There is, therefore, from B. C. 4004 to the year 1789, a great cyclical period of 5792 years, which is composed of 687, a perfect Cycle × 8 + that of 296, and at the end of it the Moon is fast 3 H. 39 M. 2 S. 39 TH. Now, this unexpected coincidence happily affords us an opportunity of again putting to the test both systems of Chronology. According to the Septuagint, Lamech was born in B. C. 4005, and, consequently, the Hebrew year of Creation, B. C. 4004, is, as has been already shown, in the Greek the 2d of Lamech. Reckoning, from

* The first attack made upon my conclusions was on this very ground, that it was *unjust to suspect the Jews*. On this point I have even had to bear the language of objurgation. The reader will, therefore, bear with me in somewhat dilating on this argument.

† See that Work, p. 32.

that year, a series of Cycles,—the following results present themselves :—

EVENTS.	DATES B.C.	CYCLICAL INTERVALS.	AT THE END OF EACH PERIOD. Moon fast.	Moon slow.
The Creation in the Hebrew Chronology,—in the Greek the 2d of Lamech,	4004			
The birth of METHUSELAH in the *Hebrew*,—in the *Greek*, the birth of JAPHET,	3317	687		H. M. S. TH. 0 10 43 41
The conception of Peleg, in the Greek,—in the Hebrew *no era at all*,	2687	630	H. M. S. TH. 6 1 33 4	
The 31st year of the Exodus, and 10 years before the entrance into Canaan; in the Greek also, 60 Jubilees from the death of Adam, B. C. 4549, and 1 square of 19 from the death of Abraham, B. C. 1970; but in the Hebrew *no era at all*,	1609	1078		5 26 19 29
The 1st Jubilee year from the Exodus, 3 years after the division of the lands, in the Greek,—in the Hebrew *no era*,	1590	19		2 4 5 35
Jerusalem taken by Nebuchadnezzar,	588	1002	2 50 2 51	
Total period,		3416	1 10 27 10	

From B. C. 588 to 1789 is the Cycle of 2376 years, at the end of which the Moon is fast 2 H. 28 M. 35 S. 29 TH. It is composed of 2080 + 296. The whole period from B. C. 4004 to 1789 is 5792 years, and at the end of it the Moon is fast 3 H. 39 M. 52 S.

I proceed to remark that even here in the series of Cycles, calculated from Usher's era of Creation, we have new evidence of the truth of the Septuagint Chronology. The three links in the Greek series, which are not found in the Hebrew at all, and especially the remarkable era, B. C. 1609, which is 30 years complete from the Exodus, and 10 years before the entrance into Canaan, afford irrefragable evidence that the whole series belongs to the Greek, as the original and true Chronology. Thus, wherever the disciples of the learned Prelate Usher turn, we drive them from their strong-holds, and take possession of them. I add one remark—Does the reader think that the fact of the birth of METHUSELAH being placed in the *Hebrew* Chronology, in the exact year of the birth of JAPHET, in the *Greek*, is the effect of chance? No. Doubtless we may discern in it another of the evidences of the deep subtlety with which the corruption of the sacred times was carried into effect. The selection of a date so conspicuously marked as the 2d year of Lamech for their era of Creation, was certainly the result of the same deep contrivances; and these things afford evidence, that the mode in which the Scribes proceeded was this:—They first fixed some of their great eras, for example, of Creation and the birth of Methuselah, taking them from real periods in the *original Chronology*, and then they pared down the generations to correspond with the outline they had first devised. By these means, though they have swept away the characters of variegated and deeply contrived harmonies which distinguish all the great series of time that form parts of the original, they have yet contrived, that some of their curtailed series should contain the shadow of these things. It is only by placing the original and the corrupted series side by side, that we see at once the wide difference between the order of time ordained by the Creator, and that devised by the creature, to tarnish the glory and corrupt the truth of the work of God.

I shall, before closing this argument, offer some further evidence to establish the truth of the remarks made in the last paragraph. I have shown in my "Synopsis of Chronology," and also in these pages, that there is in the Greek Chronology, a remarkable concentration of the times of the world towards the year 1789, the beginning of the French Revolution, evidently marking it as a great period in the dispensations of the Almighty. I have discovered, also, that, in the Hebrew Chronology, there are *four periods*, from the births and deaths of the Patriarchs, measured by the Cycle of 19, which come out in the year 1789, although, according to the doctrine of human chances, only *two such periods* ought to come out. The four are as follows:—

Events.	Dates in Hebrew Chronology.	Intervals to the year 1789.		Remarks.
	Years B.C.	Years.	Cycles of 19.	
The death of Seth,	2962	4750	250	The interval between these two dates is 20 Cycles.
The death of Jared,	2582	4370	230	
The birth of Terah,	2126	3914	206	From the death of Jared 24 Cycles.
The death of Serug,	1955	3743	197	From the birth of Terah 9 Cycles.

Before we proceed to the investigation of this series, let us inquire what are the intervals between the same points of Chronology in the Septuagint, and to what dates series of the Cycles of 19 arrive, if computed from them. They are as follows:—

1. The death of Seth was B. C. 4337, and a series of 322 Metonic Cycles from it comes out in 1782, being 46 weeks of 19, and carried on to 1820, it is 12 × 27 = 324 and in 1839 it becomes 25 × 13 = 325 Cycles.
2. The death of Jared was B. C. 3557, being, from the death of Seth, 780 years, or 41 Cycles and 1 year; and from this date a series of 281 Cycles comes out in 1783, and carried forward to 1859 it is 285, or 15 squares of 19.
3. The birth of Terah is B. C. 2215. The interval from the death of Jared is 1342 years or 70 Cycles and 12 years, and from this date a series of 210 Cycles, or 30 weeks of Cycles, expires in 1776.
4. The death of Serug was B. C. 2094, from the death of Seth it is 2243 years, or 118 Cycles and 1 year, and from that of Jared 1463 years, or 77 Cycles, being 11 weeks of Cycles. A series of 204 Cycles, or 12 × 17, comes out from this date in 1783.

I think, in contemplating the facts now set before him, the attentive reader will be forced to yield to the conviction that the Rabbis must have been perfectly aware of the existence of the Metonic Cycle, as one of the elements of the sacred Chronology, and that in curtailing it they had regard both to the Jubilee and the Cycle. How are we otherwise to account for the fact, that the interval in the Greek Chronology, between the deaths of Seth and of Jared, being 41 Cycles and 1 year, the length of the same interval in the shorter Chronology is exactly 20 Cycles, showing that 21 Cycles and 1 year has been taken from it, in order to bring the two events into one series of that Cycle? How are we also, on any other hypothesis, to account for the other fact, that there being from the death of Jared to that of Serug, in the Greek Chronology, 1463 years, or 77 Cycles, the same period is in the Hebrew exactly 33 Cycles, showing that just 44 Cycles have been abstracted from it? To the same cause we may assign the fact, that they have brought in the birth of Terah into this series of Metonic Cycles, to which it does not belong; viz. a desire to strengthen the evidence of their Chronology.

It will be necessary, in the next place, that I should give an outline of the great series of Metonic Cycles in the Greek Chronology, which comes out in the year 1789, that the reader, comparing it with that which has been shown to exist in the Hebrew Chronology, may for himself decide which is the truth. The series consists altogether of 384 Cycles, or 12 × 32, from B.C. 5470, being 8 years from Creation, to the year 1827;* but as I have not found any event or era, particularly marked in it, till the death of Noah, B.C. 2867, I shall only compute it from that era to 1789:—

Events.	Dates. Years B.C.	Intervals. Years.	Cycles. of 19.	Remarks.
The death of Noah,	2867			To the French Revolution, 1789, are 245 Cycles, or 95 Jubilees.
The death of Shem,	2715	152	8	The Chronology of these 3 eras to the French Revolution thus divides itself: The death of Shem to the birth of Abraham 30, thence to that of David 55, thence to 1789, 152 Cycles. From the death of Arphaxad 28 + 55 + 152, and of Cainan 25 + 55 + 152. All these subdivisions are perfect numbers.
The death of Arphaxad,	2677	38	2	
The death of Cainan,	2620	57	3	
The birth of Abraham,	2145	475	25	The birth of Abraham is from the death of Noah 722 years = 38 Cycles, or 2 squares of 19,—from that of Shem 30 Cycles, of Arphaxad 28, all perfect periods.

* See Introductory Dissertation to the Fulness of the Times, p. 14.

Events.	Dates. Years B.C.	Intervals. Years.	Cycles of 19.	Remarks.
The death of Joseph,	1784	361	19	One square of 19, and from the death of Noah 3 squares.
The birth of David,	1100	684	36	From the death of Noah 93 Cycles, of Shem 85, or 17 × 5, of Arphaxad 83, of Cainan 80, and the birth of Abraham 55, or 11 × 5.
The first Passover in Jerusalem, which was taken from the Jebusites the year before,	1062	38	2	From the death of Noah 95 Cycles, or 5 squares of 19,—from that of Arphaxad 17 × 5 = 85 Cycles,—from the birth of Abraham 3 squares,—from the death of Joseph 2 squares of 19.
The 1st year of the captivity of the Tribes beyond Jordan,*	739	323	17	From the death of Noah 112 Cycles, or 7 × 16,—from that of Arphaxad 17 × 6 = 102,—from the birth of David 1 square of 19.
The 1st year of the captivity of the 10 Tribes of Samaria,	720	19	1	From the death of Cainan 100 Cycles, the birth of Abraham 75, and of David 20. From the 1st Passover in Jerusalem 18 Cycles.
The 1st Passover after the desolation of Jerusalem by Nebuchadnezzar,	587	133	7	Being 1 week of the Cycle of 19; and from the death of Noah 120 Cycles, of Shem 112, of Arphaxad 110, the birth of Abraham 82, the death of Joseph 63, or 7 × 9, the birth of David 27, and the 1st Passover in Jerusalem 25 Cycles.
	After Christ.			Cycles of 19.
The French Revolution,	1789	2375	125	From the death of Noah 7 × 35 = . . . 245 Of Shem 30 + 55 + 152 = ... 237 Arphaxad 28 + 55 + 152 = ... 235 Cainan 25 + 55 + 152 = ... 232 From the birth of Abraham 55 + 152 = 207 From the death of Joseph 36 + 152 = . . 188 From the birth of David, 8 squares of 19 = 152 From the 1st Passover in Jerusalem, . . . 150

* If, as is probable, they were led captive towards the end of B.C. 740, then the year following is reckoned the first of the captivity. The same remark applies to the era of the captivity of Samaria.

Events.	Dates. Years A.C.	Intervals. Years.	Cycles of 19.	Remarks.	Cycles of 19.
				From the 1st year of the captivity of the tribes beyond Jordan, 7 squares of 19 = ...	133
				From the 1st year of the captivity of Samaria 12 × 11 = ...	132
				From the 1st passover after the destruction of Jerusalem by Nebuchadnezzar 5 × 5 × 5, or the Cube of 5 = . . .	125
The death of the Duke of York, heir apparent of the crown; the dissolution of the great Tory and war administration of Great Britain, by the illness of Lord Liverpool; the death of Mr Canning; the treaty of London between Russia, France, and England, acknowledging the independence of Greece, and the battle of Navarino,	1827	38	2	From the birth of Abraham 11 squares of 19 =	209
				The death of Joseph 10 squares = . . .	190
				The birth of David 7 × 22 = ...	154
				The 1st passover in Jerusalem 8 squares of 19 =	152
				The captivity of the tribes beyond Jordan 27 × 5 = ...	135
				The 1st passover after the destruction of Jerusalem by Nebuchadnezzar,	127
The year 1846, shown in my "Fulness of the Times" to be a great era, being, from our Lord's death on the Cross, 37 Jubilees,	1846	19	1	From the death of Noah 13 squares of 19 = .	247
				From the birth of Abraham 7 × 30 = . .	210
				The birth of David, being $5 + 5^2 + 5^3 =$	155
				The 1st passover in Jerusalem 17 × 9 = .	153

As the two Chronologies, the Greek and Hebrew, meet in B.C. 810, the date of the accession of Uzziah, it hence follows that the last part of this series of Metonic Cycles, viz., from the captivity of the Tribes beyond Jordan, B.C. 739, to the year 1789, and thence to 1846, is common to both Chronologies. It becomes necessary, therefore, to carry up the series to the earlier ages of the Hebrew Chronology, in order to discover whether in that scheme it harmonizes as well with the later eras as in the Greek. Now, let it be first observed, that none of the earlier events of this series, according to the Greek Chronology, from the death of Noah to the first passover in Jerusalem, are found in the same series, if computed according to the Hebrew Chronology. The events which form parts of the Hebrew series are those mentioned already,* whereof the relations to the parts of the series which are common to both Chronologies, are as follows: their distance in time from the French Revolution has been given above:

		Cycles of 19.
The death of Seth in the Hebrew scheme is, B.C. 2962	Thence to the captivity of the Transjordanite tribes, B.C. 739,	117
	To the captivity of Samaria, B.C. 720	118
	To the 1st Passover after the first destruction of Jerusalem, B.C. 587, ...	125
The death of Jared, B.C. 2582	Thence to the captivity of the Transjordanite tribes, ...	97
	Do. of Samaria 14 × 7 =	98
	To the year B.C. 587, . . .	105
From the birth of Terah to these three periods are,	to the 1st,	73
	the 2d,	74
	the 3d,	81

And from the death of Serug are 64, 65, and 72 Cycles.

I have now discovered that Usher's date of the finishing of the Temple, B. C. 1005, comes also into this Series, being from the death of Seth 103 Cycles, from that of Jared 83, the birth of Terah 59, and the death of Serug 50 Cycles, none of which periods, however, except the last, are perfect.

It cannot be denied, that in this Series we see further evidences of the profound artifices of the framers of the Hebrew Chronology. Yet, if the impartial reader will carefully compare the Greek and Hebrew Series, he will not hesitate in pronouncing the former to be the original Chronology. The first event in it, viz., the death of Noah, is connected with no less than three other great eras, viz., the birth of Abraham, the death of Joseph, and the 1st Passover in Jerusalem, by the square of 19. It is connected with a fourth era, that of the captivity of the Transjordanite tribes by the perfect period of 7 × 16 = 112 Cycles; and with a fifth, the 1st Passover after the destruction of Jerusalem, by another perfect period, 12 × 10 = 120; and finally, with the French Revolution by the Jubilee and Cycle united and multiplied by

* See p. 48.

5 = 95 of the former, and 245 of the latter. Now, that such a series of time should have been effected by forgery, which, be it observed, remained ignorant of the happy effects of its own devices, since these results were never seen till the present moment,* were a supposition about as absurd as the Epicurean theory of the universe.

In the next place, there is not, reckoning from the first era in the foregoing *Hebrew Series*, viz., the death of Seth, one period, measured by the *square* of 19, or by *sevens* or *twelves* of that number. The sum total of this Series, to the year after the desolation of the first Temple, is indeed a complete period, being the cube of 5, or 125; and when it reaches 1789, it is 250. But the way in which these perfect periods are obtained is very simple. The Scribes were, as will be proved below, well aware of the perfect series of Cycles from the death of Noah to B.C. 587, and having mutilated it by their corruptions, they have substituted for it their own spurious series from the death of Seth, and have placed his death just 5 Cycles, or 95 years, above the date of the death of Noah, *in the original Chronology*, and therefore in the same series of Cycles; and they have thus imparted to their own falsehood part of the characters of the original verity; for, to 120 Cycles the interval, as we have seen, from the death of Noah to B.C. 587, adding 5, the sum is their complete number of 125 from the death of Seth. But as the subdivisions in their spurious series do not exhibit the harmonies of number, the lack of this betrays the fraud.

Let it be further observed, that the exact truth of the Greek Chronology of the death of Noah, is proved not only by the series of Metonic Cycles already given, but also by a most perfect Jubilean series, beginning at the death of Seth, of which the following is a summary:—

* They were in part brought to light in my Strictures on Mr Bickersteth's Scheme of Scripture Chronology,—Introductory Dissertation to Fulness of Times, page 33.

Events.	Dates. Years B.C.	Intervals. Years.	Jubilees.	Remarks.
The death of Seth,	4337			
The death of Noah,	2867	1470	30	These two periods are each complete, and being added, are 12 × 4 = 48, a perfect number.
The birth of Jacob,	1985	882	18	
The division of the lands,	1593	392	8	From the death of Seth to the division are 7 × 8 = 56 Jubilees, or 8 cubes of 7.
The 1st Passover of the 2d Temple,	515	1078	22	This period is a Cycle, the Moon being slow 5 H., 26 M., 19 S. Also, from the death of Noah to this era are 48 Jubilees.

It will be observed, that all the intervals in this period are in themselves complete, and that, in combination, they afford two periods measured by 12, the number of the Sanctuary, and one by 7. The whole Series comes out in the present year, and will be brought before the reader in treating of its Chronology.

In the Hebrew Chronology there is no *Jubilean* series from the death of Seth to the 1st Passover of the second Temple, for it will be found, that the interval between them is 2447 years, being 3 years short of 50 Jubilees. But as the Jewish Scribes were perfectly aware of the existence of the foregoing perfect series in the original Chronology, and saw the necessity of some series of Jubilees from such an event as the death of Seth, they have, with profound artifice, placed that event, in the Jubilean series of the national Chronology, exactly 24 Jubilees below the 1st of Nisan, after the death of Enos, B. C. 4138, and beginning of the administration of the former Cainan,—21 Jubilees from the 1st of Nisan after the translation of Enoch, B. C. 3991, and 27 Jubilees before the Exodus, B. C. 1639; and by this act of chronological legerdemain, they get a perfect period of 2401 years, or 49 Jubilees = 7 cubes of 7 from their date of the death of Seth, B. C. 2962, to the liberty of Jehoiachin, B. C. 561. But the utter spuriousness of this Hebrew date of the death of Seth will be established to the satisfaction of every impartial reader, by comparing the foregoing perfect series in the Greek Chronology with that which results from the Hebrew, and is as follows:—

Events.	Dates in the Hebrew Chronology.	Intervals. Yrs.	Jubs.	Yrs.	Remarks.
The death of Seth,	2962				In the Greek Chronology, two different Series of Jubilees run from the deaths of these two patriarchs. The interval between them is 4 Jubilees and 2 years. See my Fulness of the Times, Tables, pp. 167* and 182.
The death of Enos,	2864	98		2	
The birth of Jacob,	1836	1028	20	48	And from the death of Seth 22 Jubilees and 48 years; the same interval being measured in the Greek by the perfect number of 48 Jubilees.
The division of the lands,	1445	391	7	48	From the death of Seth 30 Jubilees and 47 years; the same interval in the Greek being the perfect period of 8 cubes of 7, or 56 Jubilees.
The liberty of Jehoiachin,	561	884	18	2	From the death of Seth 49 Jubilees, or 7 cubes of 7.

The foregoing are the only eras, nearly Jubilean, which I have discovered in this Hebrew series; but it will be seen, that though the sum total of years is a perfect period, only one of the intermediate intervals is exactly Jubilean. The series is, therefore, utterly spurious. I shall confirm this conclusion, by informing such readers as are unacquainted with my former Works, that in the Greek series, from which the Rabbis have stolen their spurious date of the death of Seth, we have, from the 1st of Nisan after the death of Enos, to the same date after the translation of Enoch, 3 Jubilees, thence to the Exodus 48, thence to David's birth 11, and thence to the liberty of Jehoiachin 11, and the last two numbers form the Cycle of 1078 years; all these periods are perfect. The series begins, as I

* In the title of Table III., p. 167, at the top of the page, the name Seth is, by mistake, printed instead of Enos.

have endeavoured to show, in the Introductory Dissertation to the "Fulness of the Times," in B.C. 5461, the date, as I suppose, of the Fall, whence, to the Baptism of our Lord, are 112 Jubilees, or 16 Cubes of 7, and from the 1st of Nisan, after the death of Enos, 85, or 17 × 5 Jubilees. This series, being the truth, exhibits the features of harmony and lucid order, which are the attributes of truth.

It is time now to draw to a close this most painful discussion; but before doing so I shall very briefly demonstrate, that the Rabbis were, as I have already asserted, perfectly aware of the existence of the series of Metonic Cycles, beginning at the death of Noah, going down to the 1st Passover in Jerusalem, and thence to the 1st Passover after the destruction of Jerusalem by Nebuchadnezzar. This will appear evident from the following statement of the actual Hebrew Chronology of this period, wherein they have preserved the wrecks of that perfect series of Cycles. I shall place the Greek Chronology opposite to it for the convenience of the reader:—

	In the Hebrew Chronology.				In the Greek Chronology.		
		Intervals.				Intervals.	
	Years B.C.	Years.	Cycles. C.	Yrs.	Years B.C.	Years.	Cycles.
The death of Noah,	1998				2867		
The birth of Abraham,	1996	2	0	2	2145	722	38
The death of Joseph,	1635	361	19	0	1784	361	19
David born,	1085	550	28	18	1100	684	36
1st Passover in Jerusalem,	1047	38	2	0	1062	38	2
Total from the death of Noah,		951	50	1		1805	95
1st year of the captivity of the Transjordanite tribes,	739	308	16	4	739	323	17
1st Passover after the destruction of Jerusalem,	587	152	8	0	587	152	8
			74	5			120

It will be observed, that in the Hebrew series there are, from the death of Noah to the 1st Passover in Jerusalem, exactly 50 Cycles and 1 year. It is therefore manifest, that in shortening the period, it was their intention to preserve a series of Cycles, and they consequently were perfectly aware that in the original Chronology this period was measured by that Cycle. Now, in curtailing it they have, by an unequalled perversion of truth and probability, as well as the whole narrative of the book of Genesis, reduced the first interval from the death of Noah to the birth of Abraham, from 2 squares of 19 to 2 years, cutting off 720 years. In the 2d and 4th intervals the original Chronology is preserved untouched, the 3d interval is reduced from 36 Cycles to 28 and 18 years. After the date of the 1st Passover in Jerusalem, the series of Metonic Cycles disappears; for if from that Hebrew date we carry down the series, it arrives at the years B. C. 748 and 591, which are no eras at all. It is, however, found again at the 1st Passover of the second Temple, B. C. 515, which is from that of the first Temple in this series, B. C. 1047, exactly 532 years, or 28 Cycles, making the whole period, from the death of Noah to the former era, 1483 years, or 78 Cycles and 1 year; or, to the year B. C. 516, when the second Temple was finished, exactly 78 Cycles, or 12 × 6½.

It was then apparently the object of the scribes to make out that number of Cycles, from the death of Noah to the finishing of the second Temple, instead of the perfect period of 48 Jubilees, measuring to the year following, in the original Chronology. But there is not a perfect interval in the series, from its commencement to the birth of David, except the one which is measured by the square of 19, and is common to it with the Greek. The whole period also, of 78 Cycles, being neither divisible by 12 nor 7, is imperfect. On the other hand, in the Greek series each interval is perfect, as is observed in a former page,* and the sums total are equally perfect. Let the reader then decide which of the two schemes is stamped with internal evidence of truth.

I shall suppose twelve upright men, disciples of the Hebrew Chronology, to be enclosed in a jury-box, and required to return their verdict on oath; I therefore ask for their verdict:

* Pp. 52—54.

1. Which of these two series of Cycles, from the death of Noah, is entire and perfect, and which mutilated and imperfect? 2. Is the entire and perfect, or the mutilated and imperfect, the original Chronology—the order of time ordained by the Creator?

It becomes necessary, however, that, before I draw this discussion to an end, I should add yet further to the mass of evidence, in support of the Septuagint Chronology.

Seth died in B. C. 4337, towards the end of the year. The following year, B. C. 4336, is therefore the first of the administration of Enos; and I have found a great series of Cycles, beginning from that era, which contains the following results:

EVENTS.	DATES. Years B.C.		CYCLICAL INTERVALS.	At the end of each period Moon Fast.	Moon Slow.
The 1st year of the administration of Enos in the Greek. In the Hebrew, 332 years before Creation.	4336				
				H. M. S. TH.	
The birth of Shem in the Greek, —*in the Hebrew no era.*	3315		1021	0 45 57 16	
The birth of Nahor,—*no era in the Hebrew.*	2294		1021	0 45 57 16	
					H. M. S. TH.
The birth of Judah,—*no era in the Hebrew.*	1903		391		5 15 35 48
	After Christ.				
The treaty of Passau restores liberty to the Protestants of Germany, which is the resurrection and ascension of the Apocalyptic witnesses.	1552	These two sums, 3454 + 315, form the perfect Cycle of 3769 years, from the birth of Judah to the end of Daniel's 1335 years, the Moon, at the end of it, being only 3 M., 2 S., 32 TH., fast.	3454		2 57 44 0
The end of Daniel's 1335 years.	1867		315	3 0 46 32	
At the end of			6202		3 40 38 44

In the Hebrew Chronology, the 1st of the administration

of Enos, is B. C. 2961, and the birth of Shem, B. C. 2446, the difference being 515 years. Thence to the birth of Nahor, B. C. 2155, are 291 years; and thence to the birth of Judah, are 316 years. Now, not one of these periods is cyclical. The difference between the two Chronologies, at the birth of Shem, being, however, exactly 869 years, which has, in a former page, been shown to be an imperfect Cycle, it results from its error as there given,* that the period, from his birth in the Hebrew Chronology, to the end of Daniel's 1335 years, viz. 1867, is also very imperfectly cyclical. It is the sum of 4312 years, consisting of the Cycle of 1040 × 4 = 4160 + 19 × 8 = 152; and at the end of it the Moon is slow 21 H., 45 M., 17 S., 56 TH.; so that it is not properly a Cycle.

I have found, lastly, that from the birth of Shem, B. C. 3315, to the nativity of Christ, B. C. 3, being 3312 years, is exactly the square of 12 multiplied by 23; and it will be recollected, that from the birth of Enos to the conception of Christ, B. C. 4, are 1260 × 4 = 5040 years, or 35 squares of 12.

I now leave these results, as well as those previously arrived at, to the consideration of the intelligent and impartial reader, presuming that he will intuitively see, that the Chronology from which they flow must be the order of time ordained by the Creator of the universe.

* See page 30.

CHAPTER II.

ON THE GREAT PERIODS WHICH TERMINATE IN, AND MARK, THE YEAR 1838, OR YEAR OF THE WORLD 7316, AS THE POINT OF TIME THAT SUMS UP AND CONCENTRATES, AS IN A FOCUS, THE CHRONOLOGY OF ALL PAST AGES, AND APPEAR TO SHOW THE APPROACH OF THE END.

In my Chronology of Israel, published in the year 1835, I laid down in the body of the Work the whole Scriptural times, from the Exodus to the destruction of Jerusalem by the Romans; and in the Preface there is a summary of the Chronology up to the era of Creation, which is placed by me in B. C. 5478. With the exception of 1 year in the era of our Lord's nativity, and 2 years in the date of Herod's death, the former being brought down from B.C. 4 to 3, and the latter from B. C. 3 to 1, and also some slight corrections of the eras of the Syrian kings, for which I am indebted to the profoundly learned work of Mr Clinton, my scheme of Chronology has undergone no change since the publication of that work; and in my "Synopsis of Chronology," it is established by evidence, which I believe cannot be shaken.

It was not, however, till the following year, 1836, that I began to discern the deep wisdom of the Creator, manifested in the structure of the Chronology. In my "Fulness of the Times," published in that year, proceeding in the way of strict Chronological induction, and founding my computations upon dates of Scriptural history already known, from which I reckoned back to the age of Moses, I established the facts that, beginning at different points of time, in the period from the Exodus to the division of the lands, which comprehends, from B. C. 1639 to 1593, the sum of 46 years, there are SEVEN different series of 70 Jubilees, each of which expire at corresponding and correlative dates in the period from 1792 to the present year 1838, comprehending also 46 years, the former of which, viz., 1792, is shown in my Prophetical works to be the era of the Seventh Trumpet, and the end of Daniel's periods of 1260, and 2300 years.

It was next shown by me that the period of 70 Jubilees, in each of the seven series, subdivides itself into three intervals of 22, 12, and 36 Jubilees; the first of 22 Jubilees, being the Astronomical Cycle of 1078 years, measuring the time from the era of the Exodus and the division of the promised land, to the deliverance from Babylon; the second of 12, the time from that deliverance to the opening of the Christian dispensation, and the judgment on the Jewish nation; and the third of 36 Jubilees, the period from the baptism of Christ and the judgment on the Jews, to our own times, from 1792 to 1838.

The dates when these seven series of 70 commence, are the years B. C. 1639, that of the Exodus,—1634, the 6th of the Exodus,—1614, the 26th,—1609, the 31st of that period,—1599, the entrance into Canaan,—1596, the 4th year of the war of Canaan,—and 1593, the date of the division.

The years when they expire are:—

I. 1792. The date of the fall of the French monarchy, and the great war of the Revolution.

II. 1797. The peace of Campo Formio, being the first pause in that war.

III. 1817. The beginning of the evacuation of France by the Allied powers, and the publication of the Hebrew New Testament for the Jews.

IV. 1822. The beginning of the dismemberment of the Ottoman empire by the Greek Declaration of independence. The first converted Jewish Missionary appears at Jerusalem, preaches Christ in the Synagogues, and distributes the New Testament in Hebrew. The first preaching of the gospel to the great Jewish population of Poland, Prussia, and Russia.* The end of Daniel's 1290 years.

* This fact is established by the following words of the Report of the

V. 1832. The overthrow of the Ottoman power in Palestine and Syria, and defeat of the Grand Vizier by Ibrahim Pacha, at Koniah. The passing away of the ancient prescriptive constitution of England by the Reform Bill.

VI. 1835. The last change of administration in Great Britain, the great seat of the Church, being the fourth in the space of less than a year; and it is effected by the defeat of Sir Robert Peel's administration in the House of Commons, upon questions of ecclesiastical finance, closely connected with the temporal provision for the Protestant church in Ireland.

VII. 1838. Being 70 Jubilees from the division of the lands by Joshua,—48 Jubilees from the 1st Passover in the second Temple, and 36 from the 1st Passover after the termination of the war, and sale of the lands to strangers, by order of the Emperor Vespasian.

The dates when the various subdivisions of 22, 12, and 36 Jubilees come out, in each of the SEVEN SERIES, were imbodied by me in a short Synopsis in the above work, and as it enables me to place them before the reader in the shortest possible space, I shall transfer it to these pages, with some of the remarks that follow it:—

"SYNOPSIS

OF THE SEVEN STREAMS OF SEVENTY JUBILEES, SHOWING THE YEARS OF THE COMMENCEMENT AND END OF THEIR VARIOUS SUBDIVISIONS.

	PERIOD OF 1078 YEARS.		PERIOD OF 12 JUBILEES.		PERIOD OF 36 JUBILEES.		71st JUBILEE.	
	BEGINS.	ENDS.	BEGINS.	ENDS.	BEGINS.	ENDS.	BEGINS.	ENDS.
	Years B. C.	Years B. C.	Years B. C.	Years A.C.	Years A.C.	Years A.C.	Years A.C.	Years A.C.
I. SERIES.	1639	562	561	27	28	1791	1792	1840
II. SERIES.	1634	557	556	32	33	1796	1797	1845
III. SERIES.	1614	537	536	52	53	1816	1817	1865
IV. SERIES.	1609	532	531	57	58	1821	1822	1870
V. SERIES.	1599	522	521	67	68	1831	1832	1880
VI. SERIES.	1596	519	518	70	71	1834	1835	1883
VII. SERIES.	1593	516	515	73	74	1837	1838	1886

London Jewish Society for 1838, being their 30th. Page 56. "The "Missionary exertions of the Society are only of sixteen years standing; "*for it was not till* 1822 that the journeys amongst the great Jewish "population of Poland, Prussia, and Russia commenced."

"If the reader will next turn back to the former chapters, where the events which distinguish the various eras of the whole *seven series* are detailed, he will see that the *first* may properly be called the INITIATING, and the *seventh* the FINISHING SERIES, by which I mean that the *first*, in each of its subdivisions, *begins* a work, which, after going through various gradations in the *intermediate series* towards completion, is at length *finished* in the *seventh series*, in which series also, each of the subdivisions introduces a dispensation consequent to the one previously ended.

Thus, in the first year of the *first series*, B. C. 1639, God *began* the great work of establishing Israel as a nation and a Church, by bringing them out of Egypt. In the year B. C. 1593, the 1st of the *seventh* series, the same work was *finished* by the dividing among Israel, by the hand of Joshua, the promised inheritance of Canaan.

2d. In the year B. C. 562, which is the 1078th year of the *first* series, Nebuchadnezzar died, and in him fell the glory and power of *Babylon*. In the year B. C. 516, which is the 1078th year of the *seventh* series, *Babylon* was taken the *second* time by Darius Hystaspes, *its gates and walls demolished*, and 3,000 of its people impaled. In the same year the SECOND TEMPLE was *finished and dedicated*.

3d. The year B. C. 561, which, in the *first* series, is the 1st year of the *second subdivision* of 12 Jubilees, was also the 1st year of the liberty of Jehoiachin from prison. The year B. C. 515, being in the *seventh* series the 1st year of the 12 Jubilees, is the year of the first Passover after the dedication of the SECOND TEMPLE.

4th. The year A. C. 27, the last of the 12 Jubilees in the *first* series, is the era of the beginning of the ministry of John the Baptist. In A. C. 73, the last year of the 12 Jubilees in the *seventh* series, the whole lands of Judea were, by order of Vespasian, sold to strangers.

5th. In the year A. C. 28, which, in the *first* series, is the 1st of the 36 Jubilees, *our Lord was baptized* of John in Jordan, and with the Holy Ghost. The year 74 being in the *seventh* series, the 1st of the 36 Jubilees, and also the year after the sale of all the lands of Judea, is properly the era of the *final dispersion* of the Jewish nation. The judgment on them was now *finished.*

6th. In the *first* series, the year 1791, which is the last of the 36 Jubilees, is the period of the maturity of the first stage of the French Revolution, when it yet bore the aspect of good. In this year the king accepted the constitution, and the legislative assembly met. This was also the year of the convention of Pilnitz, which was the germ of the coalition of Europe against France. The year 1837, the last of the 36 Jubilees in the *seventh* series, is yet future.

7th. In the *first* series, the 1st of the 71st Jubilee, was the year 1792, when the Seventh Apocalyptic Trumpet first sounded at the fall of the French monarchy, and when the French Revolution put off its meretricious smiles of peace, good will to men, and was unmasked and revealed in all its horrors, as the third awful Wo of the Apocalypse. The 71st Jubilee year of the *seventh* series being 1838, is still in the womb of futurity.

I fear that some readers may complain of so much repetition in these details; but I am not aware how subjects so difficult as those which are here discussed, can be clearly exhibited without much repetition.

I shall now state, that from the whole of what has been placed before the reader, and a minute examination of the characters of the events distinguishing the various past eras of the *seventh* series, I deduce the chronological COROLLARY, that the years 1837 and 1838 are stamped with characters, the former of *finishing* and *completion*, the last of *beginning* and *restitution*,* and *re-creation.* At the moment that this is written, we are still in 1835, which does not, according to Jewish computation, end till the 17th March, 1836. Already the year 1835 has been marked as an era by the acceleration of the political drama in this country, and the utter abortion

* I use the word in the sense of Acts iii. 21; the Greek is ἀποκατάστασις.

of the endeavour to establish a conservative ministry under the new constitution, which is itself in a state of transition, and will scarcely bear any treatment but the whip and spur. This political essay, to put *old wine* in *new bottles*, seems to have failed no less egregiously than that which we are assured, by infallible authority, must always fail of putting *new wine* in *old bottles*.* The Peel conservative ministry fell in April, 1835, whether to rise again, or finally, the events of the next session will probably determine. But, be this as it may, the *sixth* series of Chronology to which the year 1835 belongs, as the 1st year of the 71st Jubilee, being one, not of a *final*, but of an *intermediate* character, the events which have already occurred in this year, are sufficiently important to distinguish it as a crisis."

Such were my conclusions two years ago, when that Work was composed. Now, without pretending to justify every expression made use of, or to say that events have gone on with the exact degree of speed I then anticipated, I must still say, that I am as fully persuaded, at the present moment, of the substantial accuracy of my principles of chronological reasoning, as I was when that volume was published. I have since found other great series of time, unknown to me when I laid down these seven series, coming out at the various points when they expire, especially the years 1817, 1822, 1832, 1835, and 1838. For those coming out in 1817, I refer to the Preface to my Fulness of the Times, pp. viii. and ix. and to the former part of this Work.† The series, coming out in 1822 and 1832, will be found in the places of my Works referred to in the foot-note;‡ and the stupendous series of Cycles, arriving at 1835, has already been given in this Work.§

Having offered these introductory observations, I shall next

* The ancient bottles were made of leather. † Page 26.

‡ For those in 1822, see the Preface to the Fulness of the Times, pp. vii. and viii.; and in the Supplementary Dissertation, p. 79; for those in 1832, see ibid., pp. 67, 70, 75, and 78.

§ Page 18.

place before my readers a Table of the great periods which terminate in the present year, and shall afterwards offer some further remarks upon them. It will be found, that some of the periods of Metonic Cycles, which are in this Table stated to be perfect periods, are, in my Fulness of the Times, given as imperfect. This, however, and other similar discrepancies, admit of an easy explanation in my more perfect acquaintance with the subject at present, than when that Work was published. This progress is so continual, that I shall have to explain certain discrepancies in the pages even of this Work, arising from some discoveries made since the first sheets were printed.

Some, however, may be inclined to say, before going further in this inquiry, that it is at least certain that the author's anticipations, with respect to the past year, 1837, have proved utterly fallacious, for that year has not proved itself to be one of finishing and completion, all things continuing even now as they were when it commenced. My answer to this is, that if 1838 shall pass away without any event connected with the opening of the dispensation of the age to come, then this objection will prove true, but not otherwise; for by a year of finishing or completion, I mean the last year which *terminates*, leaving things in their *former state*.

I have yet one introductory observation to the Table to offer, and it is to say, that there will be found in it a repetition of much that is contained in the Table of Metonic Cycles from Creation, which has been placed before him in pp. 11—15 of this Work; and some readers may be dissatisfied with this. It, however, has appeared to me, on the whole, to be more advisable to enlarge the Work by a very few pages of such repetitions, than to send the reader back to former parts of it at every step of the inquiries, and the more so, as I have some thoughts of publishing this chapter as a separate Tract.

THE GREAT PERIODS OF CHRONOLOGY WHICH EXPIRE IN THE YEAR 1838, OR YEAR OF THE WORLD 7316, COMPUTED AS ENDING ON THE DAY AFTER THE VERNAL EQUINOCTIAL NEW MOON, OR MARCH 15TH, 1839.*

Events.	Dates. Years B.C.	Length of each period to 1838.	Remarks explanatory of the periods, and showing their connexion with other great eras.
1. The Creation,	5478	7315	This great period, comprehending the whole sum of mundane time from the Creation to this year, is *most perfect:* it is 385 Cycles of 19, or 19 × 7 = 133 × 11 = 1463 × 5, being 55 *weeks*, or 11 × 5 of the Metonic Cycle. If carried on another Cycle, it becomes *imperfect.*
2. The birth of Enoch,	4357	6194	Being 326 Cycles of 19. This period, as to its sum total of Cycles, which is not divisible by 7, 12, 5, or 4, is *imperfect.* But if subdivided, it becomes perfect. 1st, From the birth of Enoch to the Deluge, are 12 × 5 = 60 Cycles of 19, a perfect number; and thence to 1838, are 14 squares, that is, 2 weeks of squares of 19. Or, 2dly, Reckoning from the birth of Enoch to the death of Christ, his resurrection and ascension, A.C. 33, the whole period is the week of the Metonic Cycle, or 133 × 11 = 1463 × 3 = 4389 years; and thence to 1838, are 5 squares of 19. In either way this period is in its component parts *most perfect.*
3. The death of Seth,	4337	6174	Being 18 Cubes of 7, or 126 Jubilees, a most perfect period.
4. The death of Enos,	4139	5976	This period is equal to 41½ squares of 12. It also divides itself as follows:—1st, To the birth of Ishmael, B.C. 2059, is the Cycle of 1040 × 2 = 2080. Thence to B.C. 1019, the Consecration of the First Temple, 1040 years; and thence to 1838, the sacred number, 12 × 17 = 204 × 14 = 2856 years.

* I have not calculated the exact time of this New Moon. But I see, by the Jewish Almanack for their year 5599, that the 1st of Nisan next is on March 16th.

THE GREAT PERIODS OF CHRONOLOGY WHICH EXPIRE

Events.	Dates. Years B.C.	Length of each period to 1838.	Remarks explanatory of the periods, and showing their connexion with other great eras.
5. The year before the translation of Enoch, being the last he finished upon earth, and in preaching to the children of men,	3993	5830	A perfect Cycle, being 1040 × 5 = 5200 + 630, at the end of which the Moon is slow 29 M., 8 S., 31 TH. The death of Abraham, B.C. 1970, is from this date 2023 years, a Cycle, the Moon fast 3 H., 36 M., 0 S., 7 TH. The birth of Joseph, B.C. 1894, is from it 2099 years, a Cycle, the Moon slow 4 H., 40 M., 22 S. The foundation of the Second Temple, B.C. 520, is from it 3473 years, a Cycle, the Moon slow 5 H., 1 M., 49 S.
6. The Deluge,	3217	5054	Being 266 Cycles, or 14 squares of 19. From Creation to the Deluge is the week of the Metonic Cycle × 17 = 119 Cycles, a perfect period: from the birth of Enoch to this great era are 60 Cycles; from the death of Seth it is 40 × 4 = 160 weeks = 1120, and from the translation of Enoch it is 6 cubes, and 1 square of 5 = 775 years.
7. The death of Noah,	2867	4704	Being 49 × 12 = 588 × 8, that is, the Jubilee multiplied by the number of the Church, 12, and again by 8, the first cube above unity, = 96. This number is, therefore, most perfect, and it is bisected by the year B.C. 515, the first Passover of the Second Temple.
8. The birth of Eber,	2820	4657	This number is an imperfect Cycle, consisting of two more perfect: 1st, we have 2300 years from the birth of Eber to the foundation of the Second Temple, B.C. 520, the Moon fast 10 H., 44 M., 57 S.; and thence to 1838, the Cycle of 2357 years, the Moon fast 4 H., 32 M., 41 S.
9. The foundation of Babel or Babylon,	2400	4237	Being 223 Cycles of 19, an imperfect number; but in its subdivisions, 1st of 98 Cycles = 7 × 7 = 49 × 2, or 38 Jubilees, to the taking of Babylon by Cyrus, B.C. 538, and thence to 1838, the period of 125 Cycles, this period is most perfect. My reasons for fixing this date will be found in the Preface to my Synopsis, pp. xviii., xix.

IN THE YEAR 1838, OR YEAR OF THE WORLD 7316.

Events.	Dates. Years B.C.	Length of each period to 1838.	Remarks explanatory of the periods, and showing their connexion with other great eras.
10. The 2d year of its building being the year before the confusion of tongues,	2399	4236	The Cycle of 353 years, at the end of which the Moon is slow 1 H., 7 M., 24 S., 38 TH., multiplied by 12.
11. The covenant of circumcision, the conception of Isaac, and the destruction of Sodom,	2046	3883	The Cycle of 353 × 11, or 7 + 4, being, from the preceding era, 1 Cycle of 353.
12. Isaac in his 7th year, Ishmael cast out,	2039	3876	204 Cycles of 19, or 17 × 12.
13. The birth of Jacob,	1985	3882	78 Jubilees, or 6½ twelves. The fraction of 6 Jubilees leads us to the 30th year of Moses, B.C. 1691. Thence to 1838, are 72, or 6 twelves, of the Jubilee; and hence we learn, that from the death of Noah to Moses' 30th year, are 2 twelves of the Jubilee.
14. The death of Abraham,	1970	3807	A Cycle composed of that of 1040 × 3 = 3120 + 687, the Moon at the end of it slow 4 H., 5 M.
15. The birth of Reuben,	1907	3744	The square of 12 = 144 × 26, or 2 cubes + 2 squares of that number. The birth of Reuben, the FIRST-BORN of Israel, is a great era. In virtue of the covenant, he was the heir of the promise, that Messiah should come from his loins; but he lost it by his sin, and the BIRTH-RIGHT, to a double portion (See Deut. xxi. 17) of the promised land, passed to Joseph, the first-born of Rachel, of whom came, accordingly, two of the twelve tribes of Israel,—Ephraim and Manasseh. (1 Chron. v. 1.)
16. The birth of Joseph,	1894	3731	The Cycle of 334 × 10 = 3340 + 391, the Moon fast at the end of it 4 H., 11 M., 13 S., 42 TH. From this date, to the foundation of the Second Temple, B.C. 520, is the Cycle of 1374 years, the Moon slow 21 M., 27 S., 22 TH.

THE GREAT PERIODS OF CHRONOLOGY WHICH EXPIRE

Events.	Dates. Years B.C.	Length of each period to 1838.	Remarks explanatory of the periods, and showing their connexion with other great eras.
17. Jacob arrives at Shechem,	1887	3724	196 Cycles, or 7 × 4 = 28 weeks of 19, or 76 Jubilees, a most perfect period. The arrival of Jacob at Shechem is a great scriptural era. He there purchased a parcel of a field of the land of promise, and erected an altar called El-Elohe-Israel. In my Synopsis of Chronology, this event was placed in the year of his departure from Padan-aram. For the reasons stated in page 11 of this Work, I now believe it was a year later.
18. Joseph, governor of Egypt,	1864	3701	This period is composed of a series of Cycles, viz. 353 × 10 = 3530 + 19 × 9 = 171; but it is not itself a Cycle, as the Moon is behind the Sun, at the end of it, more than a day. The sum of 353 × 9 = 3177 + the Cycle of 334 = 3511 years, leads to the peace of Westphalia, 1648, and thence 190 years to 1838.
19. The 1st year of famine,	1856	3693	A Cycle, composed of that of 2300 + 1355 = 3655 + 19 × 2, at the end of which the Moon is fast 8 H., 19 M., 24 S., 52 TH.
20. The famine ended,	1849	3686	194 Cycles of 19, an imperfect number. From this date to the death of Christ, A.C. 33, are 19 × 11 = 209 × 9 = 1881 years, or 99 Cycles of 19; and thence to 1838 are 5 squares of 19. The whole period, thus subdivided, becomes 2 complete numbers.
21. The death of Jacob,	1838	3675	75 Jubilees, or 5 × 5 = 25 × 3, —the death of Jacob is, from Creation, the Cycle of 1,040 × 3½ = 3,640 years, being 520 *weeks* of years, but not a Cycle. It is the bisecting point of time between the Creation and the beginning of the last great war of the French Revolution in 1803, and is in all respects a great era, being the passing away of the Patriarchal age.

IN THE YEAR 1838, OR YEAR OF THE WORLD 7316.

Events.	Dates. Years B.C.	Length of each period to 1838.	Remarks explanatory of the periods, and showing their connexion with other great eras.
22. The appearance of God to Moses in the Bush,	1640	3477	183 Cycles of 19, an imperfect period, but in its subdivisions perfect. From this date to the 3d of Saul, when he properly took the kingdom, are 7 × 4 = 28 Cycles, and thence to 1838 are 155 Cycles, or computing to the accession of David, B. C. 1070, it is from this era 30 Cycles, and thence to 1838 are 153. All these periods are *complete*.
23. The 2d year of the war of Canaan,	1598	3435	A perfect Cycle, the Moon slow 53 M., 38 S.
24. The division of the lands,	1593	3430	70 Jubilees, or 10 Cubes of 7.
25. The death of Joshua,	1583	3420	180 Cycles of 19, or 12 × 15, or the square of 12 = 144 × 23¾ years. My reasons for this date will be found in my Chronology of Israel, Chap. v.
26. Othniel judges Israel,	1564	3401	This period is 179 Cycles of 19, and is in its sum total imperfect. But reckoning from this date to the 3d year of Saul, B. C. 1108, we have 24 Cycles, and thence to 1838, are 155 Cycles, both which are perfect periods. Or, again, from this era to the death of Christ in 33, we have 12 × 7 = 84 Cycles, and thence to 1838 are 5 squares of 19. When thus subdivided this period is perfect; and as Othniel was the first of the judges, his administration is the epoch of that dispensation, and a great era.
27. The end of the 2d servitude under Eglon, king of Moab,	1507	3344	176 Cycles of 19, or 11 × 16, a complete period. From this era to the death of Christ are 9 × 9 = 81 Cycles, also a complete period.
28. Gideon judges Israel,	1359	3196	A Cycle, being that of 353 × 9 = 3177 + 19, at the end of which the Moon is slow 12 H., 10 M., 47 S., 17 TH.

THE GREAT PERIODS OF CHRONOLOGY WHICH EXPIRE

Events.	Dates. Years B.C.	Length of each period to 1838.	Remarks explanatory of the periods, and showing their connexion with other great eras.
29. The 3d year of Saul. 1 Sam. xiii. 1, 2.	1108	2945	155 Cycles of 19, being the root 5 + its square 25, + its cube 125, and therefore a number complete and perfect. This era is, before the death of Christ, 12 × 5 = 60 Cycles, and, as to the 3d year of Saul being the true era of his taking the kingdom—compare 1 Sam. xiii. 1, 2., and xiv. 47. There is, undoubtedly, a difficulty in xiii. 14, but we may understand that Samuel spoke prophetically, or that the exact order of time is not observed in the narrative.
30. The accession of David,	1070	2907	153 Cycles of 19, or 17 × 9.
31. The dedication of the Temple,	1019	2856	(12 × 17 = 204) × 7 = 1428 × 2 = 2856 years, being the number of the Church, 12 × 17, or 10 + 7, a number of perpetual occurrence in the Scriptural Chronology, and again by 14. This period is, therefore, complete and perfect. It is also bisected by the year 410, when Rome was taken and sacked by the Goths, under Alaric. This era is, from Creation, 13 cubes of 7, or 91 Jubilees.
32. The era of Nabonassar, and beginning of Daniel's FIRST KINGDOM,	747	2584	136 Cycles of 19, or 17 × 8, a perfect period. This era is 17 Cycles from the accession of David, and the whole period to 1838 is bisected by the last taking of Rome by the Goths. This is the real beginning of the TIMES OF THE GENTILES. Luke xxi. For the Chronological relations of this era to other great periods, see page 12 of this Work, and the remarks below.
33. The captivity by Tiglath-Pileser of the Tribes beyond Jordan,	740	2577	Equal to the prophetical period of 1260 years × 2 = 2520 + 19 × 3 = 57.
34. The captivity of Samaria and the Ten Tribes,	721	2558	The period of 1260 × 2 = 2520 + 19 × 2.

IN THE YEAR 1838, OR YEAR OF THE WORLD 7316.

Events.	Dates. Years B.C.	Length of each period to 1838.	Remarks explanatory of the periods, and showing their connexion with other great eras.
35. Babylon taken by Cyrus. The end of Daniel's FIRST KINGDOM,	538	2375	125 Cycles of 19, or 5 × 5 × 5, being the cube of 5. This era is from Creation 260 Cycles, from the foundation of Babel 7 × 14 = 98, from the appearance of God to Moses 58; the 3d of Saul 30, the accession of David 7 × 4 = 28. This date also bisects the whole period from the death of Noah, B. C. 2867 to the year 1792, the end of Daniel's 1260 years, and the era of the Seventh Trumpet of the Apocalypse.
36. The second foundation of the Second Temple. Hag. ii. 18.	520	2357	A Cycle consisting of 2080 + 277, the Moon fast at the end of it 4 H., 32 M., 41 S., 4 TH. This date is connected with the last year of Enoch, and also with the birth of Joseph, by the Cycles of 3473 and 1374 years, for the errors of which see the remarks on those eras.
37. The 1st Passover in the Second Temple,	515	2352	48 Jubilees, or 12 × 4. This great era bisects the whole period from the death of Noah to 1838. It is from the death of Seth 78 Jubilees,—from the birth of Jacob 30, and from his death 27 Jubilees, and from the division of the lands 22 Jubilees, or the Cycle of 1078 years.
38. The end of the Old Testament Canon, according to Josephus, and the death of Artaxerxes Longimanus,	424	2261	Being 119 Cycles, or 7 × 17. This is the measure also of the period from Creation to the Deluge, so that in the present year, 1838, we are distant in time from the finishing of the Old Testament Canon, the same interval, as was from Adam, till Noah entered the ark. This date, as mentioned in a former page, is, from Jacob's arrival at Shechem, 77 Cycles,—from the appearance of God to Moses at the Bush, 8 × 8 = 64,—from the 3d year of Saul 36, and from the accession of David 17 × 2 = 34 Cycles, all of which are perfect periods. It is from Creation 14 squares of 19.

THE GREAT PERIODS OF CHRONOLOGY WHICH EXPIRE

Events.	Dates. Years B.C.	Length of each period to 1838.	Remarks explanatory of the periods, and showing their connexion with other great eras.
39. The death of the usurper Bessus, and the complete subjection of Persia by Alexander the Great. This is the epoch of the dominion of Daniel's THIRD KINGDOM,	329	2166	114 Cycles, or 6 squares of 19. This era is from Creation 14 squares of 19 and 5 Cycles,—from the Deluge 8 squares of 19,—from the taking of Babylon 11 Cycles. From this date to the death of Christ is 1 square of 19.
40. Jerusalem taken by Pompey, who enters and profanes the HOLY OF HOLIES. This is the epoch of the dominion of Daniel's FOURTH KINGDOM over the CHURCH OF GOD,	63	1900	100 Cycles of 19. This great era is, from the preceding event, 2 weeks of Cycles.—It is from Creation 15 squares of 19,—from the Flood it is 166 Cycles, which period is bisected by God's appearance to Moses at the bush.—It is, from Jacob's arrival at Shechem, 12 × 8 = 96 Cycles.
41. Julius Cæsar assassinated in the Senate House,	44	1881	99 Cycles of 19, or 11 × 9.
42. The Death, Resurrection, and Ascension of Christ,	After Christ. 33	1805	Being 95 Cycles, or 5 squares of 19. (Cycles) This greatest of eras is from Creation 15 squares of 19, and 5 Cycles = ... 290; The birth of Enoch 33 weeks of Cycles = . . . 231; The Deluge 9 squares of 19 = ... 171; The appearance of God to Moses 11 × 8 = ... 88; The 3d of Saul 12 × 5 = 60; The taking of Babylon, . 30; The end of the Old Testament Canon, ... 24; The end of Persia 1 square of 19 = ... 19
43. The triumph of Vespasian and Titus for the Jewish war, when the spoils of the Temple were exhibited in the streets of Rome to the gaze of the populace,	71	1767	93 Cycles of 19, or 31 × 3.
44. The end of the Jewish war by the taking of Massada,	73	1765	The Cycle of 353 × 5 = 1765 years, being 7 of that Cycle from the 2d year of the building of Babel, and 6 from the destruction of Sodom and conception of Isaac. This is the last year of 42 Jubilees, or 6 Cubes of 7 from the birth of Jacob.

IN THE YEAR 1838, OR YEAR OF THE WORLD 7316.

Events	Dates. Years A. C.	Length of each period to 1838.	Remarks explanatory of the periods, and showing their connexion with other great eras.
45. The martyrdom of Polycarp,	166	1672	Being 19 × 11 = 209 × 8, or 88 Cycles. This date bisects the period from the end of the 2d Servitude under Eglon.
46. The great irruption of the Huns into Europe, from the North of China, which, in the following year, precipitates the Goths on the Roman empire,	375	1463	77 Cycles of 19, or 7 × 11, and as the period from Creation to 1838 is 1463 × 5, it follows that this period is the last 5th part of the whole mundane ages to this year.
47. The great Theodosius, for the last time, unites the whole Roman empire a few months before his death,	394	1444	Being 76 Cycles, or 4 squares of 19. Cycles of 19. This great era is from Creation 16 squares of 19 and 5 Cycles = ... 309 The birth of Enoch . . 250 The Flood, 10 squares of 19, 190 The foundation of Babel 57 Jubilees, or . . . . . . 147 Jacob's arrival at Shechem 120 The accession of David 7 × 11 = ... 77 The era of Nabonassar 12 × 5 = ... 60 The taking of Babylon 19 Jubilees, ... 49 The end of Persia, 2 squares of 19, ... 38 The taking of Jerusalem by Pompey, ... 24
48. The taking and sacking of Rome by Alaric and the Goths,	410	1428	Being 12, the sacred number × 17 = 204 × 7, or 1 Septenary of that number. This great era bisects the whole period from the dedication of the First Temple to 1838. It is also a great Jubilean period from the birth of Shem and other great eras, as will be shown below.
49. The last taking of Rome by the Goths,	546	1292	Being 17 × 4 = 68 Cycles of 19. This is the bisecting point from the era of Nabonassar to 1838. It is from the Deluge, 11 × 18 = 198 Cycles of 19; from the accession of David, 17 × 5 = 85 Cycles; and from the death of Christ, 27 Cycles.

THE GREAT PERIODS OF CHRONONOGY WHICH EXPIRE

Events.	Dates. Years A.C.	Length of each period to 1838.	Remarks explanatory of the periods, and showing their connexion with other great eras.
50. The siege of Rome by Astolphus and the Lombards, raised a second time by Pepin, mayor of the palace of France, who gives possession to the Pope of several towns, and next year cedes to him the exarchate of Ravenna. This is the epoch of the temporal power of the Popes,	755	1083	Being 57 Cycles, or 3 squares of 19; and the bisection of the whole period from the end of Persia, B.C. 329. This great era is, from Creation, 17 squares of 19 and 5 Cycles, or — Cycles. 328 From the Deluge, 11 squares, or . . . . . . 209 From the accession of David, 12 × 8, or . . . 96 From the death of Christ, 2 squares of 19, or . . . 38
51. The death of Charles the Gross, who reigned nearly over the whole Empire of Charlemagne, which is followed by the dismemberment of the Empire into five states,	888	950	Being 19 × 50; and the bisection of the whole period, from the taking of Jerusalem by Pompey.
52. Charles the Bold, duke of Burgundy, killed at the siege of Nancy. His daughter and heiress, Mary, married on the 18th or 20th of August, to Maximilian of Austria. Their son Philip, 19 years afterwards, viz. 1496, espouses Joan, heiress of the Spanish monarchy,	1477	361	Being 1 square of 19. This era is from Creation, the cube of 19 and 5 Cycles, being — Cycles. 366 From the Flood, 13 squares of 19, being . . . . . 247 From the finishing of the Old Testament Canon, 100 From the death of Christ, 4 squares of 19, ... 76
53. The massacre of the Protestants on St Bartholomew's day, in France. War of the United Provinces against Spain renewed; the assembly of the States at Dort and Haerlem; the siege of Haerlem,	1572	266	14 Cycles of 19.
54. Henry IV. of France abjures the Protestant faith,	1593	245	5 Jubilees.
55. The civil war begins in England,	1642	196	4 Jubilees.

IN THE YEAR 1838, OR YEAR OF THE WORLD 7316.

Events.	Dates. Years A.C.	Length of each period to 1838.	Remarks explanatory of the periods, and showing their connexion with other great eras.
56. The complete subjection of Ireland, and the treaty of Limerick, establishing the Protestant ascendency,	1691	147	3 Jubilees.
57. The accession of Maria Theresa of Austria leads to a general European war,	1740	98	2 Jubilees.
58. The French Revolution,	1789	49	1 Jubilee.

In order to obtain an adequate view of this stupendous chain of time, covering the whole period from the day when Adam was made a living soul to the present year, it becomes necessary to classify the various eras comprehended in it. They may, perhaps, be fitly arranged as follows:—I. Great MUNDANE ERAS, ancient and modern. II. Great PATRIARCHAL ERAS. III. Great ERAS of the MOSAIC DISPENSATION not classed under the former heads. IV. Events intermediate, and of secondary importance.

I. 1. Under the *first* head, we find first the era of Creation; whence to the present year, 1838, are 7315 years, or 55 weeks, of the Cycle of 19. The number 55, or 11 × 5, will be found in the Chronology, as the measure of various great periods. Thus, from the birth of Enos, B. C. 5044, to the end of the Jubilee of the division of the earth, B. C. 2349, being 2 years before the death of Peleg, are 55 Jubilees. From the death of Adam, B. C. 4549, to the settlement of Israel in Goshen, B. C. 1854, is the same period of 55 Jubilees. From the birth of Arphaxad, B. C. 3215, to the foundation of the Second Temple, B. C. 520, are 55 Jubilees. From the birth of Abraham, B. C. 2145, to that of David, B. C. 1100, is the same number of Metonic Cycles.

This great period, which is thus shown to be perfect as a sum total, divides itself in various ways, its subdivisions being likewise complete and perfect numbers. *First*, It is the *week of the Metonic Cycle*, 133 years × 11 = 1463 × 5 = 7315. Its highest factor is, therefore, 1463, which, being the multiple of the *week* of 19 by 11, is most perfect.

Secondly. This period divides itself as follows:—

1. From the Creation to the Deluge, are 2261 years, or the Cycle of 19 × 7 × 17 = . . . 119 Cycles.
2. Thence to the finishing of the Old Testament Canon, and death of Artaxerxes Longimanus, B. C. 424, are 57 Jubilees, or . . 147 —
3. Thence to 1838, ... 119 —

Each of these subdivisions is in itself a complete number, and the first and second, and second and third, are equally the sum of 7 × 2 = 14 squares of 19, which number is most perfect.

Thirdly. This period may be subdivided:—

1st. From Creation to the taking of Jerusalem by Pompey, B. C. 63, whereby were fulfilled the words of Daniel viii. 10, are 5415 years, or 15 squares of 19 = 285 Cycles.

2d. Thence to 1838 is the perfect number of a century of Cycles, or 1900 years, . . 100 —

Thus, in whatever mode this great period is subdivided, it is perfect as a whole, and perfect in its subdivisions; but if carried on a single year further, and made 7316 years, it loses all these properties and becomes imperfect, not being divisible by 7, or 12, or 5, or 19; and if carried on another Cycle of 19, it is made 386, which number also being divisible neither by 7 or 5, nor even by 4, is imperfect. Moreover, consisting, as this period does, of 5 times 1463 years, that number cannot occur again till the year of Christ, 1838 + 1463 = 3301.

2. The *second* great mundane period in this series is the ERA OF THE DELUGE, whence the interval of 14 squares of 19 to 1838, is most perfect.

It subdivides itself in various ways. *First*, as already mentioned, under the *second* head of the former mundane period, from the Deluge to the finishing of the Old Testament, and thence to 1838.

Secondly. 1st. From the Deluge to the appearance of God to Moses, are . . . . . 83 Cycles of 19.

2d. Thence to the taking of Jerusalem by Pompey, ... 83 ——

3d. To 1838, ... 100 ——

266

The two first numbers of 83 Cycles are imperfect; but then the exact subdivision of the whole period, from the Deluge to the taking of Jerusalem, by the great era of the appearance of God to Moses, makes up for this defect.

Thirdly. This great period divides itself into 9 squares of 19, from the Deluge to the death of Christ, and thence to 1838, 5 squares.

3. The *third* great mundane period is that of the foundation of Babel, B. C. 2400. The period thence to 1838, being 223 Cycles, is imperfect; but being divided, we have, to the accession of David, B.C. 1070, the sum of 1330 years, or . . . . 70 Cycles,
and from that era, 17 × 9, ... 153 —

Both these subdivisions of the period are complete, and the former most perfect.

Secondly. From the foundation of Babel to the death of Christ, A.C. 33, we have 8 × 8 = 64 × 2 = 128 Cycles;
and thence to 1838 are 5 squares of 19, or 95 —

In either way the subdivision exhibits perfect periods.

Should any reader inquire what are my reasons for placing the foundation of Babel in B.C. 2400, and what is the evidence which supports it, I must refer him to my Synopsis of Chronology, Preface, pp. xviii—xxii. I may, however, in my turn, rather put the question to the disciples of Usher,—on what evidence they rest their chronological and moral paradox, that Babel was built, according to Usher, B. C. 2247, or, according to the last version of his Chronology, in Y. W. 1850, being B. C. 2157, and in the former case 249, and in the latter 150 years before the death of Noah. As well might men, in the present day, publish books to prove that the earth is a *cube*, as to tell us that, consistently with the verity of the narrative of Genesis, the building of Babylon was during Noah's life. Were there no other millstone to tie round the neck of the Hebrew Chronology, this alone would sink it in the depths of the sea.

4. The *fourth* great mundane period is that of the DESTRUCTION OF SODOM, THE CONCEPTION OF ISAAC, AND THE COVENANT OF CIRCUMCISION; whence to 1838 is the Cycle of 353 years × 11. This period is therefore complete; and from this date to the taking of Massada, and end of the Jewish war, A.C. 73, are 6 Cycles of 353. This measure of time cannot again occur till the year of Christ 2191.

5. The *fifth* great mundane era is that of the appearance of God to Moses, which, subdivided as in the column of Remarks, is perfect. Also, from B.C. 1640 to the death of Christ, A.C. 33, are 11 × 8 = 88 Cycles; and thence to 1838, 5 squares of 19,—both periods being complete.

6. The *sixth* mundane era is that of the accession of David, whence, to the present year, there are 9 periods of 323 years, being the Metonic Cycle multiplied by 17. This period is therefore complete.

7. The *seventh* mundane period is the era of Nabonassar, B. C. 747, the beginning of the kingdom of Babylon, and it may, in the comprehensive sense of the words, be considered as the beginning of the TIMES OF THE GENTILES, spoken of by our Lord in Luke xxi. 24, for within 7 years of this date, viz., B. C. 740, the Transjordanite tribes were carried captive by Tiglath-Pileser, king of Assyria; and within 26 years, viz. B. C. 721, the Ten Tribes of Samaria were carried captive by Shalmanasar. The TIMES OF THE GENTILES, beginning at this great era, and computed to the year 1838, include the sum of 19 × 17 = 323 × 8 = 2584 years, being 136 Cycles, which period is bisected by the last taking of Rome by the Goths, in the year 546. This period is complete and perfect.

		Cycles.
This great era is, from Creation,	. . . .	249
	The birth of Enoch 10 squares of 19, or	190
	The Deluge, ...	130
	Jacob's arrival at Shechem, . . .	60
	The 3d year of the Servitude of Moses 19 Jubilees, or	49
	The 3d year of Saul, 1 square of 19, or	19

8. The *eighth* great mundane period is the taking of Babylon, B.C. 538, whence, to 1838, is the Metonic Cycle multiplied by the Cube of 5 = 125. This period is also in its subdivisions perfect. 1st. From the taking of Babylon to the 3d year of the administration of Nehemiah, when it is probable that some of his great administrative reformations were completed, are 5 Cycles; 5, as the multiple of 19, being the root of the whole period to this year. 2d. The square of 5 leads us to the taking of Jerusalem by Pompey, B. C. 63, which is 25 Cycles from the taking of Babylon. 3d. The root 5 + the square 25 = 30 Cycles, leads us from the taking of Babylon to the death of Christ,—whence to 1838 is the square of 19 multiplied by the root 5. The whole Chronology of this period is, therefore, a continued series of the Cycle of 19 multiplied by 5, and arranged with the deepest artifice.* For the relations of this era to the other great periods of Chronology, I must refer to the column of Remarks.

9. The *ninth* great mundane period is the complete subjection of Persia by Alexander the Great, and the death of the Usurper Bessus, B. C. 329, whereby the empire of Alexander was firmly established. This is the epoch of the dominion of Daniel's THIRD KINGDOM. It is from Creation 14 squares of 19 and 5 Cycles, and from the Deluge 8 squares. From the era of Nabonassar 22, and the taking of Babylon 11 Cycles of 19.

10. The *tenth* mundane era is the taking of Jerusalem by Pom-

* See the Supplementary Dissertation to my "Fulness of the Times," pp. 63—66, where will be found a detailed view of the structure of this part of the Sacred Chronology, computed from the siege of Babylon by Cyrus, B.C. 540 to 1836, which is equally applicable to the period from the taking of Babylon to 1838.

pey, B. C. 63, by which event the FOURTH KINGDOM OF DANIEL placed its feet on the neck of the captive and prostrate church and kingdom of Israel, which was the antithesis of Josh. x. 24. This event is, from Creation, 15 squares of 19. Thence to 1838 are 100 Cycles.

11. The *eleventh* in this series, and greatest of all mundane periods, is that of the DEATH, RESURRECTION, and ASCENSION of CHRIST, whence to 1838 are 5 squares of 19 years. It is, from Creation, 15 squares and 5 Cycles of 19, and from the Deluge 9 squares. For its relation to the other great eras of the world, I refer to the Table of Remarks.

12. The *twelfth* great mundane era is the year 375, that of the irruption of the Huns from the north of Asia into Europe, driving before them the Goths, whom they, in the following year, precipitated on the Roman empire.

From this era to 1838 are 19 × 7 × 11 = 1463 years, or . . . . 77 Cycles.

It is from Creation 44 weeks of 19, or 1463 × 4, or . . . . 308 —

From the Deluge, 27 weeks of 19, or . 189 —

From the accession of David 4 squares of 19, or 76 —

From the taking of Babylon by Cyrus 12 × 4, 48 —

And from the death of Christ, . . 18 —

13. The *thirteenth* great mundane era is the reunion, for the last time, of the whole Roman empire, under Theodosius the Great in 394,—from which to the present year, are 4 squares of 19. I refer to the column of Remarks for the other particulars of its chronology. It is, from the era of Nabonassar, 60 Cycles of 19.

14. The *fourteenth* mundane era is the taking of Rome by the Goths, under Alaric, in 410, whence to 1838, are 1428 years, being 12 × 17 = 204 × 7; or the number of the church, 12 multiplied by 17, and again by 7 the perfect number; or it may be stated as 12 × 7 = 84 × 17. This great era bisects the whole period from the dedication of the first Temple, B. C. 1019 to 1838. It is from Creation 841 weeks of years, or 120 Jubilees and 7 years; from the birth of Shem,

B. C. 3315, it is the perfect period of 76 Jubilees, or 196 Metonic Cycles, being 28 weeks of that Cycle; from the Deluge, 74 Jubilees; from the entrance of Vespasian into Galilee with the Roman army in the year 67, it is 7 Jubilees, or 1 cube of 7. The eras of Shem and of the entrance of the Roman army, under Vespasian, into Palestine, which are not included in the Table, are thus brought into chronological connexion with the present year.

15. The *fifteenth* great mundane era is that of the second entrance of Pepin, Mayor of the palace of France, into Italy in 755, and raising the siege of Rome by Astolphus and the Lombards. I refer to the column of Remarks for its chronological relations to other great eras. It is from the taking of Babylon by Cyrus, 17 × 4 = 68 Cycles of 19, and from 755 to 1838, are 3 squares of 19.

The whole remaining periods given in the Table being eight from No. 51 to 58, may be considered as great mundane eras; but I must refer to the Table for them, as it would extend these observations to too great a length were I to notice them particularly.

II. I now come to the second class, or the great patriarchal periods, in this stupendous series of time.

1. The *first* is the birth of Enoch, B.C. 4357, from which era the series of 326 Cycles of 19 to the present year, though in its sum total it is imperfect, yet when divided in either of the modes stated in the column of Remarks, it becomes perfect. I shall now add, that it is capable of being divided in a third way. From the birth of Enoch to the era of Nabonassar, B.C. 747, are 3610 years, or 10 squares of 19, and thence to this year 17 × 8 = 136 of that Cycle. When thus subdivided the whole period is also perfect; but if we carry it on one other Cycle of 19, viz. to the year 1857, it becomes imperfect, whether the point of subdivision be the Deluge or the era of Nabonassar. On the other hand, if the death of Christ be the point of subdivision, we still have, from that great era to 1857, the perfect number of 12 × 8 = 96 Metonic Cycles, less perfect, however, than the 5 squares of 19 which

come out this year. It follows, therefore, from the whole of these results, that the year 1838 is the point of time when the Chronology, from the birth of Enoch, is summed up, and concentrated with the other great periods of time, in a common focus.

2. The death of Seth, B.C. 4337, is the *second* great patriarchal era connected with 1838, the period being 18 cubes of 7, which is altogether perfect. It is bisected by the year B.C. 1250, the middle of the administration of Jephthah. In the year 1789, that of the French Revolution, this series was 5 × 5 × 5, or the cube of 5 = 125 Jubilees, a perfect number. If, again, we carry it on to the year of Christ 2181, we have then 19 cubes of 7, or 133 Jubilees, or 343 Metonic Cycles = 6517 years, which is also itself a perfect Cycle, the Moon slow 39 M., 52 S.; and this, probably, is one of the most remarkable periods among the scientific numbers, as uniting the cube of 7, the Cycle of 19, and Cycles of Astronomy. I shall, however, next observe, that neither in 1789 nor 2181, have we the series of Jubilees from the death of Noah measured by 12, which comes out in 1838; nor have we in either of those years the great periods of Metonic Cycles, which terminate in the present year. It is therefore evident, that the year 1838 is the true point of concentration of the Chronology from the death of Seth.

3. The *third* patriarchal era is the death of Enos, B.C. 4139, whence the interval to 1838 is 41½ squares of 12, which, in its sum total, is imperfect, but divided as stated in the column of Remarks, it forms a series of complete time.

4. The *fourth* patriarchal era is the last year which Enoch completed upon earth, or the year before his translation, being B.C. 3993. The period is measured by one of the most perfect Cycles.

5. The *fifth* patriarchal era is the death of Noah, B.C. 2867, the period from which, to 1838, is 12 × 8 = 96 Jubilees, being bisected by the 1st Passover in the Second Temple, B.C. 515. This measure of the Jubilee cannot occur again till the year of Christ 1838 + 588 = 2426; and as it then

will not meet the series of the cubes of 7 from the death of Seth, or of Metonic Cycles from Creation, it follows that the year 1838 is its point of fulness and concentration.

6. The *sixth* patriarchal era is the birth of Eber, B.C. 2820.

7. The *seventh* patriarchal era is the 7th year of Isaac, B.C. 2039, when Philo tells us he was weaned. In my Fulness of the Times, I stated on the authority of Dr Gill, that, according to Philo, he was weaned a year later, or at 7 years complete; but I have since found the passage in his writings, and I think its import is, that Isaac was in his 7th year, and not 7 complete;* for in the context, Philo says that Ishmael was then about 20. Now, that this is a great scriptural era is manifest, for we have thence to the Exodus, B. C. 1639, the exact period of 400 years, which is revealed to Abraham, Gen. XV. 13. and therefore appears to be dated from the casting out of Ishmael. From this era to the 7th year of Christ, we have also the perfect Cycle of 2042 years, the Moon fast 1 H., 31 M.

The series of time, which runs from this date to 1838, being the Metonic Cycle × 17 = 323, and again multiplied by 12, is perfect; and it touches the great eras of the accession of David, B. C. 1070; of Nabonassar, B. C. 747; of the finishing of the Old Testament Canon, B. C. 424; and of the last taking of Rome by the Goths, A. C. 546. As it is measured by the perfect number 12, this year is evidently its point of *fulness.*

8. The *eighth* patriarchal era is the birth of Jacob, B. C. 1985
9. The *ninth* the death of Abraham, 1970
10. The *tenth* the birth of Reuben, 1907
11. The *eleventh* the birth of Joseph, 1894
12. The *twelfth* the arrival of Jacob at Shechem, 1887
13. The *thirteenth* the exaltation of Joseph in Egypt, 1864
14. The *fourteenth* great patriarchal era is the death of Jacob, 1838

* His words are περι δε την επταετιν ἡλικιαν παυσαμενῳ της εν γαλακτι τροφης εκεινῳ. Philo. Opera, tom. i. p. 393, Mangey edition. Usher places the weaning of Isaac in his 5th year, if I rightly understand the learned prelate, who, in fixing dates, often studies obscurity.

With this event the patriarchal ages passed away; and its date equally bisects the whole period from the Creation, B. C. 5478, to the beginning of the last great war of the French Revolution in 1803.

III. Under the *third* general head of great periods of the Mosaic dispensation, not classed in the second, we enumerate the following:—

1.	The 2d year of the war of Canaan, . .	B. C. 1598
2.	The division of the lands, ...	1593
3.	The death of Joshua, ...	1583
4.	The administration of Othniel, the beginning of the dispensation of the Judges, ...	1564
5.	The last year of the 2d Servitude under Eglon,	1507
6.	The administration of Gideon a great era, being a special type of the miraculous deliverance of the Church at the second advent of Christ, . .	1359
7.	The 3d year of Saul,—the era when he really took the kingdom. Compare 1 Sam. xiii. 1. with xiv. 47, ...	1108
8.	The dedication of the Temple, ...	1019
9.	The captivity of the tribes beyond Jordan by Tiglath-Pileser, ...	740
10.	The captivity of the ten tribes by Shalmanasar,	721
11.	The second foundation of the Second Temple,	520
12.	The 1st Passover in the Second Temple, . .	515
13.	The end of the Old Testament Canon, . .	424
14.	The triumph of Vespasian and Titus, . .	A. C. 71
15.	The end of the Jewish war, ...	73

The foregoing three classes, comprehending 23 + 14 + 15 = 52 different eras, leave only 6 of the whole number of 58, included in the series, to be classed, as of an *intermediate* and *secondary* character, and they are those numbered in the Table, 10, 19, 20, 41, 45, 49. It may however be doubted, whether the last ought not rather to have been included in the great mundane eras.

I now proceed briefly to draw the attention of my readers to the great divisions of time which measure these great ages of the world:—

1. We have, on the basis of the Metonic Cycle, 11 weeks of that Cycle, being 1463 years.

This number, multiplied by 5, is the measure of the whole of the mundane ages to this year; and 5 is, as I have shown in my former Works, the root of the whole of the times of the kingdom of Israel, as the multiple of the Metonic Cycle.*

The number 1463 is also the measure of the period, marked 46, and also of the whole time, from the birth of Enoch to our Lord's death on the cross.

2. The periods 2, 6, 39, 42, 47, 50, and 52, being seven in whole, are measured by the square of 19, or . . . . 361 years.
This number also measures many of the intermediate periods, and it pervades the whole Chronology.

3. Three periods being 3, 24, and 37, are measured by the cube of 7, or series of 7 Jubilees, ... = 343 —

4. The periods 12, 30, 32, 38, and 49, by the Cycle of 19 multiplied by 17, . . = 323 —

5. Periods 25 and 26, by the same Cycle, multiplied by 12, ... = 228 —

6. Periods 20, 27, 41, and 45, by the same, multiplied by 11, ... = 209 —

7. Periods 4 and 15 by the square of 12, . = 144 —

8. Periods 22 and 53 by the week of 19, . = 133 —

9. Periods 29, 35, 40, and 51, by the Cycle of 19, multiplied by 5, and its multiples 25, 125, 150, and 155, which last being $5 + 5^2 + 5^3$, is the fulness of that number.

10. Period 21 by the Jubilee, multiplied by the square of 5, ... = 1225 —

11. Periods 10, 11, and 44, by series of the Cycle of 353.

12. Periods 5, 16, and 23, by other perfect Cycles.

* See Appendix to Supplementary Dissertation to my Fulness of the Times, p. 82.

13. Periods 8, 14, 19, and 28, by imperfect Cycles.
14. Periods 18, 33, and 34, by series of larger Cycles.
15. The periods 7, 13, and 37, by the Jubilee, multiplied by 12, ... = 588 years.

Now, the very fact of the concentration in one and the same year of so many periods from the greatest eras of the world, including the CREATION, the DELUGE, and the DEATH OF CHRIST; the beginnings of the dispensation of Moses, and its end by the taking of the last fortress in Judea: also the beginning of the dispensations of the judges, and the kingdom of Israel, and of David, as well as of each of the four kingdoms of Daniel; these periods being measured by divisions of time so various, and yet all complete and perfect; these things, we affirm, afford the most irrefragable evidence, that the arrangement of the mundane ages, which produces such results, must be the contrivance of the Infinite Mind, the CREATOR OF ALL WORLDS. It indeed offers itself to my understanding as self-evident, that to suppose any manufactured or corrupted Chronology to have effected this, is as absurd—perhaps much more so—than if we were to refer the most stupendous monuments of ancient art, the ruins of Palmyra, and Tadmor, and Persepolis, not to the labours of man, or, as the eastern nations do, of genii, but of those species of the animal creation, which, in their external form, approach nearest to man.

But if I press this argument too far, then let the disciples of Usher refute it by facts. They, it seems, possess the true Chronology! incumbered indeed with a few awkward difficulties and paradoxes; as that the people, whose sins St Paul declares to have been filled up, who had crucified the Messiah, and were the persecutors of his Church, and are the chronological forgers who have corrupted the times of Daniel's prophecy of the 70 weeks, telling us in their Almanacks, as I see from that of their year of the world 5598, answering to 1837–8, now open before me, that, from the destruction of the first Temple by Nebuchadnezzar, to that of the second by the Romans, were only 490 years, the true Chronology being 657 years, are yet more worthy of credit than the apostles of the Lord, and the first churches, and the text of St Luke!——As that Abraham was born only 2 years after the death of Noah, and was the cotemporary of Shem, Arphaxad, Salah, Eber, the last of whom actually survived him; and thus that there were different and discordant economies of the world coexistent and coetaneous!——As that it is better to twist, and crucify, and reject the chronological testimony of the whole Book of Judges, than expressly to admit that the immaculate Rabbis have interpolated in a single text, 1 Kings vi. 1.—a single false number! Yet notwithstanding these few and awkward difficulties—we repeat it—the disciples of Usher can have no difficulty, seeing they possess *the truth!* in producing, from their *hidden treasures,* greater and more stupendous concentrations of the true Chronology, at some given point of time, than has now been evolved from that of the Septuagint!

I proceed next to remark, that it may easily be shown, that the year 1838, is the point of SUMMING UP, or, to use a scriptural word, of the FULNESS of all these periods. Let us select from them, as an example, the one from the accession of David, B. C. 1070, which is measured by the multiple of the Metonic Cycle by 17 = 323, and again by 9 = 2907 years, or 153 Cycles. Now, if we carry on this number another Cycle, it becomes 7 × 22, that is 22 weeks of that Cycle; and it may be justly affirmed, that this being a multiple of 19 by 7, is more perfect than the former number. Nevertheless, that the former, is the measure of the *chronological fulness* of the whole period from the accession of David, appears not only from its being a part of a series of 12, the number of fulness of the church, from the 7th year of Isaac to 1838, but also from the circumstance, that, if we compute forward to 1857, we lose all the series of Jubilean time, and also the periods measured by 1463 and 361, besides others; for, at the year 1857, the periods last mentioned become imperfect, excepting the one from the death of Christ, which is at that year 12 × 8 = 96 Cycles. As, however, in nature there are successive fulnesses: first that of the leaf, next of the blossom, lastly of the fruit; so in Chronology also, there are germinating fulnesses of the times, and dispensations of God. It is, therefore, not denied by me, that in 1857, there will be a further fulness of the times, measured from the accession of David, in confirmation of which, I shall now state, that, calculating from B. C. 1070, the date of that great event, a series of weeks of the Metonic Cycle, 4 weeks, = 532 years, bring us to the taking of Babylon, B. C. 538; thence 7 weeks, = 19 Jubilees, or 931 years, bring us to A. C. 394, the era of the last reunion of the Roman empire under Theodosius; and these two periods are equal to 1463 years. Another week, or 133 years, computed from the date last mentioned, brings us to B. C. 527, the date of the accession of Justinian, whence to 1857, are 10 weeks = 70 Cycles, or 1330 years; and the whole period, from David's accession to 1857, is the period of 22 weeks, or twice the sum of 1463 years. In order, however, yet more fully to demonstrate the nature of the fulness, or summing up of the ages, which is accomplished this year, I shall state to the reader, that I have made the calculation, when the four following series of time, which concentrate in this year, can meet again, and for greater facility of reference, I shall distinguish them by the letters A, B, C, D:—

A. That from Creation, measured by 11 weeks of 19, or	1463 years.
B. That from the Deluge and the death of Christ, of which the common measure is the square of 19, or	361 —
C. That from the death of Seth, measured by the cube of 7, ...	343 —
D. That from the death of Noah, its measure the Jubilee 49 × 12, ...	588 —

The result is, that the two first series, A, calculated from Creation, B. C. 5478, and B, from the Deluge, B. C. 3217, and the death of Christ, A. C. 33, cannot meet again till the lapse of 27,797 years after the present year; that C, calculated from the death of Seth, and D, from that of Noah, cannot again meet for 4116 years after the year 1838; and that the whole four series, A, B, C, and D, calculated from the same eras, cannot meet again till the lapse of 114,412,452 years after 1838. I presume, therefore, that, according to the doctrine of chances, the chances of these four periods from the four eras of Creation, the Deluge, the deaths of Seth and Noah, meeting in the present year, are exactly the last sum of years, minus 1 against, and 1 for it.

Were we to extend the calculation further, to find when these periods can meet, with a few of the other divisions of time, which measure the great periods expiring this year, it would produce sums of years, so entirely transcending the powers and the conceptions of the human understanding, that it were useless to pursue the inquiry. It is, perhaps, enough for us to know, that the measures of the periods from the Creation, the Deluge, and the death of Christ, cannot meet again for 27,797 years; and, therefore, it incontrovertibly follows, that they are now in the year 1838, for the first time, concentrated in one point, and summed up, and cannot again be for that immense period.

I shall remark, in drawing to a close, that there are several great periods of the world which terminate in the present year, and are not measured by scientific time, but are distinguished by their points of bisection, being great eras of history.

1. From the birth of Noah, B.C. 3817 to 1838, is the period of 5654 years, which is not divisible by 7, 5, 12, or 19, and is not a Cycle of Astronomy, but its bisecting point is the year B.C. 990, the date of the accession of Rehoboam and the rending from him the kingdom of the ten tribes.

2. From the birth of Shem, B. C. 3315 to 1838, the period is 5152 years, which is not a multiple of any of the perfect numbers, but is the 6th term of a series of geometrical proportion, of which 161 is the first term, and 2 the ratio. The series is 161, 322, 644, 1288, 2576, 5152. The 5th term being the bisection of the whole period, leads to B. C. 739, the 1st year of the captivity of the tribes beyond Jordan.

3. From the liberty of Jehoiachin to this year, are 2398 years, which period is bisected by the year 639, when the Saracens completed the conquest of Syria, having 2 years before taken Jerusalem.

I shall state finally, that in March, 1839, being the 1st of Nisan, of the year of the world 7317, we arrive at the end of the great Cycle of 7299 years from the year of the Fall, B. C. 5461; and at the termination of that great period, which consists of the Cycle of 1040 × 7 = 7280 + 19, the Moon is behind the Sun 11 H., 11 M., 3 S., 48 TH. I have, in former passages of this Work, supposed that some of my readers may dissent from my conclusion as to the date of the Fall, even if they receive my Chronology generally. I must, however, now so far qualify my former expressions as to say, that if they will ponder the mass of evidence contained in the 1st section of my Introductory Dissertation, confirmed, as it is, by the unexpected Cyclical conclusions arrived at in my Synopsis of Chronology, p. 31, and Preface, p. xx. they will, I think, find it impossible to withhold their assent to this date.

Finally, at Nisan, 1839, we arrive at the end of the perfect Cycle of 5830, from the translation of Enoch, B. C. 3992; and we are now in 1838, in the last year of both these great periods from the Fall and the translation of Enoch, and within 6 months of their termination.

It is also remarkable, that if we place the translation of Elijah in the 2d year of Ahaziah of Israel, B. C. 910, when this king probably died, we have thence to the next year, 1839, the perfect Cycle of 2748 years, consisting of 1040 + 334 × 2, at the end of which the Moon is slow 42 M., 54 S., 44 TH.; and since I began this paragraph, I find that Usher also places the translation of Elijah in the 2d of that king, which in his scheme, is B. C. 896. Concluding, therefore, that the translation of that great prophet was in the 2d of Ahaziah, which, in the true Chronology, is B. C. 910, we have, from the translation of Enoch, B. C. 3992 to that of Elijah, B. C. 910, the period of 3082 years, which is a perfect Cycle, composed of those of 1040 × 2 = 2080 + 1002, at the end of which the Moon is fast 13 M., 46 S., 13 TH.; and thence to 1838, the perfect Cycle of 2748, the Moon slow, as already mentioned, which gives the error of the whole period, from the translation of Elijah to this year, being the sum of the foregoing Cycles, or 5830 years, to be the Moon slow 29 M., 8 S., 31 TH.; and let the reader be again reminded, that we are within little more than 6 months, at the date on which this is penned,* of the time when these immense periods come to a termination.

It remains that I should briefly offer the reasons which appear to lead to the conclusion, that the stupendous series of time, terminating in the present year, is an unequivocal chronological indication of the nearness of the end. I must here, in the first place, refer the reader to my Dissertation on the Apocalypse, and the Supplement to the same, which I have lately published. In these Works it has, I think, been established, by arguments which cannot be answered, that the 1260 years of Daniel expired at the sounding of the Seventh Apocalyptic Trumpet in 1792, the 1290 years in 1822, and that the 1335 years will come out in the year 1867.

Now, as it is emphatically declared in Dan. xii. 12. that all who attain to the last period are blessed, it undeniably, I think, follows, that before then, or at that point of time, the kingdom of God, in all its blessedness, will have been established upon earth. Let us then consider, on the one hand, the brief space which separates us from that era, now only 28 years and a-half, and on the other, the mighty events which are to fill the intervening space. These are the destruction of the FOURTH KINGDOM of Daniel, or CHRISTIAN EUROPE, by judgments of the most overwhelming nature, including in them all that is written in Dan. vii. 9—14, and remains yet unfulfilled; all that is declared in Isa. xxxiv.; Jer. xxv. 27—38; and Rev. xviii. and xix.; also the restoration of the Jews; the destruction of Babylon; the rebuilding of Jerusalem; the invasion and overthrow of Gog; and the celestial events of

* September 15th, 1838.

the second advent of Christ with the clouds of heaven, and the rapture of his saints, who are to be with Him, according to the promise in Rev. ii. 26, 27. when He dashes in pieces the nations. Now, if these things are to fill little more than 28 years, it appears, at least to our humble view, necessary they should begin immediately. We are indeed aware, that the Scriptures declare that the events of the last times shall be marked, by their miraculous suddenness. "*I have long time holden my peace; I have been still and refrained myself: now will I cry like a travailing woman; I will destroy and devour at once; I will make waste mountains and hills, and dry up all their herbs; and I will make the rivers islands, and I will dry up the pools. I will bring the blind,* viz. the spiritually blind Jews, *by a way that they knew not; I will lead them in paths that they have not known; I will make darkness light before them, and crooked things straight. These things will I do unto them, and not forsake them.*"* Such are the declarations of the Lord, with respect to the things which are at the door, and which this generation shall witness. We have also, in our own times, seen the once proud monarchy of the Bourbons, which shook Europe with the terrors of its prowess, vanish from the earth in the short space of 3 years, from 1789 to 1792;—we have seen the colossal empire of Napoleon crumble to the dust, and *melt with blood*,† in the equally short period of 3 years, from 1812 to 1815; and the elder branch of the restored Bourbons fugitives from their throne and capital, in three days. These great revolutions teach us somewhat of the even more awful suddenness of the things that are coming. Yet, when we consider their complicated nature, and that it is apparent, from the words of Ezekiel, that the Jews will have dwelt in their own land for some considerable period before the invasion of Gog, we are still persuaded, that the first actings of the mighty drama must be forthwith expected.

Here, however, it will naturally be asked, what are the

* Isa. xlii. 14—16.

† Isa. xxxiv. 3.

great chronological characters which distinguish the year 1867, marking it as a great era of the Divine dispensations, and confirming the former conclusions of the author, before he knew any thing of the scientific Chronology? This question is reasonable, and has been already in part answered in the Supplement to my Dissertation on the Seals. Referring to my original Dissertation for the reasons which first led me to fix these dates, I, in the Supplement, (pp. 17, 18,) stated, that besides various great Jubilean periods which come out in 1866, the following come to an end in 1867:—

1. From the entrance of Joshua and the children of Israel into Canaan, B.C. 1599 to 1867, is the Cycle of 315 × 11, ... = 3465 years.
2. From David's carrying the Ark of God to the city of David on Mount Zion, B.C. 1060 to 1867, 11 weeks of the Metonic Cycle = 1463 × 2, 2926 ——
3. From the birth of Judah, B.C. 1903 to 1867, a perfect Cycle, the Moon fast 3 M., 2 S., 32 TH., 3769 ——
4. From the death of Noah, B.C. 2867, a Cycle, the Moon fast 7 H., 1 M., 16 S., 33 TH., . . 4733 ——

I have now to add the following Jubilean periods coming out in 1867:—

1. From the birth of Enoch, B. C. 4357, . 127 Jubilees.
2. From the birth of Reuben, B. C. 1907, . 77 ——
3. From the Administration of Othniel, the epoch of the Judges, B. C. 1564, ... 70 ——
4. From the foundation of the second Temple, B. C. 535, ... 49 ——
5. From our Lord's 7th year complete A. C. 5, 98 Cycles of 19, or . . . . 38 ——

And the following great cyclical periods:—

1. From the 1st of Nisan after the death of Seth B. C. 4336, being the first year of the administration of Enos. The Moon slow 3 H., 40 M., 38 S., 44 TH., ... 6202 Years.
2. From the birth of Shem, B. C. 3315, a Cycle, the Moon slow 4 H., 26 M., 36 S., ... 5181 ——

3. From the birth of Nahor, B. C. 2294, the Cycle of 1040 × 4, the Moon slow 5 H., 12 M., 33 S., 16 TH. 4160 years.
Lastly, from Creation, B. C. 5478, are, to 1867, exactly 51 squares of 12, ... 7344 ——

This period thus subdivides itself: 1st, from Creation to B.C. 5046, the second year before the birth of Enos, probably that of the marriage of Seth, are 3 squares = 432 years. 2d. Thence to the conception of Japhet, B. C. 3318, is the cube of 12 = 1728 years. 3d. Another cube leads us to B. C. 1590, the 1st Jubilee year after the Exodus, and 3 years after the division of the lands was begun, perhaps 1 year after it was completed; and thence to 1867, are 2 cubes of 12.

The whole of these periods evidently mark the year 1867 as a great era in the Divine dispensations, and, therefore, powerfully and irrefragably confirm my former reasoning, establishing the Chronology of the times of Daniel.

We are also now 1 Septenary of years from the entrance of the army of Egypt into Palestine, at which time, or in the following year, as I have shown elsewhere,* the warning was given to the church by our Lord himself:—BEHOLD I COME AS A THIEF, BLESSED IS HE THAT WATCHETH AND KEEPETH HIS GARMENTS LEST HE WALK NAKED, AND THEY SEE HIS SHAME.† It was then, in the primary and preparatory sense of the word, that the END began.

In the ultimate and more proper sense of the word, however, the END does not commence till either our Lord descends from heaven to gather his elect, or until the restoration of the Jews begins, whichsoever of these great events shall, in the order of time, have precedence; and with respect to this, there are different opinions even among those who receive both in a literal sense. Now, the series of times which concentrate in the present year, comprehending, as they do, the measures of all mundane, patriarchal, and Jewish ages, appear, I think, clearly to indicate the proximity of the END in this ultimate

* See Supplement to my Dissertation on the Seals, pp. 73—75.

† Rev. xvi. 15.

sense of the word. The reasons of this are, that no secondary event, even of the greatest importance, can answer to such a concentration of times from the CREATION, the DELUGE, and the DEATH, RESURRECTION, and ASCENSION OF THE LORD OF GLORY, nor any other event than his SECOND ADVENT IN GLORY. Neither can any event happen respecting the political destinies of the World, which shall be correlative to the beginning of the FIRST, SECOND, and THIRD KINGDOMS OF DANIEL, and the first subjection of the CHURCH to the FOURTH KINGDOM, but the deliverance of the Church from its subjection to that kingdom, and the beginning of the KINGDOM OF GLORY OF THE SON OF MAN. Nothing, moreover, can have an adequate co-relation to the births and deaths of so many of the patriarchs, both antediluvian and postdiluvian, from which great periods concentrate in the present and the two past years,* but their reunion in the presence of the Lord in their glorified and resurrection bodies. No other event, also, can have a co-relation to the translation of Enoch and Elijah, from which perfect Astronomical Cycles expire in March next, only six months from the moment when I write these remarks, but the translation of the SEALED SAINTS, who shall be found alive when Christ appears. I pretend not to prophesy, nor do I lay it down as a certain inference, that these events are to happen at the time marked by this great concentration of times. We must not presume to limit the HOLY ONE OF ISRAEL. He may, for reasons hidden from us, depart from the analogies of his chronological arrangements in times past. But what I do certainly infer is, that either this great concentration of the ages of the World, signifies nothing at all, as to the nature of the events that are coming, or that it must denote the approach of things, which, in transcendent moment, are correlative to, and commensurate with, the great epochs from which the various series of time are computed.

* In 1836, a period of 336 Cycles of 19, or 48 *weeks* of that Cycle, from the death of Adam, came to an end: in 1837, great Cyclical periods from the deaths of Shem, Arphaxad, and the second Cainan.

INTRODUCTORY REMARKS

TO THE

FOLLOWING TABLE.

The Septuagint Chronology is given from the Tables in my Synopsis of Chronology. The Hebrew is given according to the most accurate Table of the Chronology of Usher which I have met with. It is that which is found in Bagster's Quarto Comprehensive Bible, 1827. But I have amended one or two dates, which plainly deviate from the Tables of Usher, or from all probability. In Bagster's Table the death of Joshua is absurdly placed in B.C. 1443, only 2 years after the division of the lands. I have placed it according to the Chronology of our Bibles, in B.C. 1427. Again, Usher gives in his Annals the year of the foundation of the Temple, B.C. 1012, and places its finishing 7 years after, in B.C. 1005, both which dates are in exact harmony with his system. In Bagster's Table the foundation is placed in B.C. 1012, but the finishing B. C. 1004, which, according to this system, is a year too late.

This date I have, therefore, stated as in Usher's Annals, from which I should have preferred taking the whole of the dates directly, were it not that his Tables are in many places so confused in their arrangement, as to render it difficult to get possession of his dates.

The reader will find some eras left blank in the Hebrew Chronology, there being no dates affixed to the events in the Tables of that system. In one such case, however, viz. that of the finishing of the Ark, which is placed by me in the penultimate year of the antediluvian world, I have, though the era does not appear in Usher, supplied it according to his scheme, because it affords one of the best arguments for his system which are to be met with. See pp. 30, 31, of the 1st Chapter of this Work. Now, it is the first duty of a writer, on all subjects connected with the elucidation of Divine truth, (and none is more intimately connected with it than the Chronology,) to state fairly, and to give the utmost possible degree of weight, to the arguments of his opponents, because not to do so is *dishonest*, and we may be assured, that God will not grant to *dishonesty*, the high honour of discovering and making known the truth. Though, therefore, I have spoken with very great severity, respecting the Hebrew Chronology, in these pages, I am not conscious of having, in a single instance, kept back any evidence in its favour, from Jubilean or other scientific periods, which are the result of the deep contrivances of the Jewish Scribes. It is, indeed, not impossible I may, in some instances, have failed to discern its evidence,* and if so, the advocates of that system are sufficiently acute to discern, and will be quite as willing to proclaim to the public, wherein I have missed the truth.

I shall next state, that though I believe that Usher has been entirely deceived, in his conclusions, in favour of that Chronology, yet I willingly attribute to him the praise of having correctly apprehended, what the Hebrew Chronology really is. He has acurately given it, with one exception, which will be noticed below, as it came at first from the hands of the corrupters of the truth, in the existing Hebrew text, their present popular and still further curtailed system, being a more recent corruption, and, therefore, in his hands, it has lost none of the evidences, of deep contrivance and skill, which originally belonged to it. It is otherwise, as to the attempts of some of his disciples, who have tried to mend or patch up his scheme.

If the reader will turn back to page 36, he will there see a perfect series of Jubilees, which I view as being the master-

* In page 16, there is one instance of this; but it will be rectified in the Appendix.

piece of the Scribes. Now, I have looked into the Tables of Mr Bickersteth's new version of the Hebrew Chronology, and I find the various intervals of that series stand in it as follows. I have supplied the date of the birth of Shem, which is omitted by him, but being 100 years before the birth of Arphaxad, ought to stand in his Table, Y.W. 1559:—

	Y.W.	Intervals. Years.	Jubilees. J.	Y.
Enos born,	236			
Shem,	1559	1323	27	0
The Flood,	1656	97	1	48
Jacob's exile at Padan-aram,	2246	590	12	2
Foundation of 2d Temple in 2d of Cyrus,	3472	1226	25	1
			66	2

It will be here seen, that the perfection of the original Hebrew scheme, is lost, both in the subdivisions and in the sum total.

I have not thought it necessary to try the other periods of this scheme, since it does not appear to me, that its deviations from Usher, rest on any other authority than the imagination of its learned author. It is, however, obvious, that it loses also the evidence for Usher's scheme, from the cyclical periods coming out from his mundane era, B. C. 4004, to the French Revolution, 1789, and other intermediate eras. This it does, by placing the Creation in B. C. 4006, two years earlier, whereby it moreover loses the Jubilean and Cyclical periods which result from Usher's scheme.

I have said above, that there is one exception to the accuracy of Usher, in having correctly apprehended the Hebrew Chronology. By his mode of computing the years *Before Christ*, he really loses 1 year in the whole period, from his mundane era, to the vulgar era of the Nativity. To explain this: as his era of Creation, or year of the world 1, is B. C. 4004, it is obvious that his year of the world, 2, ought to be B. C. 4003, whereas it will be found that his tables are constructed on the principle that it is B. C. 4002. If I had taken advantage of this error, I believe it would have marred the accuracy of all his Cycles and Jubilean periods down to modern ages. For example, the great Cycle from the 2d of Lamech, B. C. 4004, to 1789, the date of the French Revolution, amounting to 5792 years, the Moon fast, as stated in page 45, more than 3 H., 29 M., does really, according to the illustrious Prelate's mode of computing the years before Christ, not come out till the year 1790. I have, however, not imputed this error to Usher, as I think it probable he did not clearly discern it. Hales, I conceive, fell into the same mistake. Had Usher seen it, he would probably have made up the defect of a year, by counting to Ahaz, 16 years instead of 15, the former being the scriptural length of his reign.* But, as already said, I have done to Usher, according to the rule of our Lord, *as I would that other literary opponents should do to me*, and have given him all the advantages in argument, resulting from his correct apprehension of the Rabbinical era of Creation, as being B. C. 4004, without noticing his deviation from it in his subsequent calculations. In so doing I have, on the one hand, placed before the reader the whole weight of the evidence, which can be brought in favour of the Hebrew Chronology, and putting in the opposite scale, the overwhelming weight of evidence, which supports the Greek, have shown that on the former is inscribed *Mene, mene, Tekel*, thou art weighed in the scales of truth and found wanting.

I have yet two remarks to make respecting the Table:—1. The difference to the Christian era is the difference of the two Chronologies at each date, which is known by subtracting the year *before Christ* of the *Hebrew* from that of the *Greek*. If the reader desires to know the difference at each date in Metonic Cycles, by dividing the sum of difference in years by 19 he will obtain it. 2. Jacob's years, when he had his children, are his age, as stated in my Table of the Septuagint Chronology. According to the dates in the Hebrew, he was 84 years at the birth of Reuben.

* See, on this point, my "Chronology of Israel," page 33, and "Synopsis of Chronology," page 21 et passim.

A COMPARATIVE TABLE OF THE SEPTUAGINT AND HEBREW CHRONOLOGIES, FROM CREATION TO THE ACCESSION OF UZZIAH, B.C. 810, SHOWING THEIR JUBILEAN DIFFERENCE TO THE CHRISTIAN ERA AT EACH DATE.

Names and Events.	Septuagint.		Hebrew.		Difference to the Christian Era.		
	Year of the World.	Before Christ.	Year of the World.	Before Christ.	Years.	Jubilees.	
						Jub	Yrs.
Adam created,	1	5478	1	4004	1474	30	4
Adam falls,	18	5461	1	——	1457	29	36
Seth born,	230	5249	130	3874	1375	28	3
Enos born,	435	5044	235	3769	1275	26	1
Cainan born,	625	4854	325	3679	1175	23	48
Mahalaleel born,	795	4684	395	3609	1075	21	46
Adam dies,	930	4549	930	3074	1475	30	5
Jared born,	960	4519	460	3544	975	19	44
Enoch born,	1122	4357	622	3382	975	19	44
Seth dies,	1142	4337	1042	2962	1375	28	3
Methuselah born,	1287	4192	687	3317	875	17	42
Enos dies,	1340	4139	1140	2864	1275	26	1
Lamech born,	1474	4005	874	3130	875	17	42
Enoch translated,	1487	3992	987	3017	975	19	44
Cainan dies,	1535	3944	1235	2769	1175	23	48
Noah born,	1662	3817	1056	2948	869	17	36
Mahalaleel dies,	1690	3789	1290	2714	1075	21	46
Jared dies,	1922	3557	1422	2582	975	19	44
Noah begins to build the Ark,	2142	3337	1536	2468	869	17	36
Japhet born,	2162	3317	1556	2448	869	—	—
Shem born,	2164	3315	1558	2446	869	—	—
Ham born,	2165	3314	1560	2444	870	17	37
Lamech dies,	2227	3252	1651	2353	899	18	17
Methuselah dies,	2256	3223	1656	2348	875	17	42
The Ark finished,	2260	3219	1654	2350	869	17	36
The Flood,	2262	3217	1656	2348	869	—	—
Noah leaves the Ark: the covenant of God with him and all flesh. Gen. ix. 9.	2263	3216	1657	2347	869	—	—
Arphaxad born,	2264	3215	1658	2346	869	—	—

A COMPARATIVE TABLE OF THE SEPTUAGINT AND HEBREW CHRONOLOGIES, FROM CREATION TO THE ACCESSION OF UZZIAH, B. C. 810.

Names and Events.	Septuagint.		Hebrew.		Difference to the Christian era.		
	Year of the World.	Before Christ.	Year of the World.	Before Christ.	Years.	Jubilees.	
						Jub.	Yrs.
2d Cainan born,	2399	3080					
Salah born,	2529	2950	1693	2311	639	13	2
Noah dies,	2612	2867	2006	1998	869	17	36
Eber born,	2659	2820	1723	2281	539	11	0
Shem dies,	2764	2715	2158	1846	869	17	36
Peleg born,	2793	2686	1757	2247	439	8	47
Arphaxad dies,	2802	2677	2096	1908	769	15	34
Cainan dies,	2859	2620					
Reu born,	2923	2556	1787	2217	339	6	45
Salah dies,	2962	2517	2126	1878	639	13	2
Serug born,	3055	2424	1819	2185	239	4	43
Eber dies,	3068	2416	2187	1817	599	12	11
Babel founded,	3079	2400	1757	2247	153	3	6
Confusion of Tongues,	3081	2398					
Peleg dies,	3132	2347	1996	2008	339	6	45
Nahor born,	3185	2294	1849	2155	139	2	41
Reu dies,	3262	2217	2026	1978	239	4	43
Terah born,	3264	2215	1878	2126	89	1	40
Abraham born,	3334	2145	2008	1996	149	3	2
Serug dies,	3385	2094	2049	1955	139	2	41
Nahor dies,	3393	2086	1997	2007	79	1	30
Abraham arrives at Haran,	3406	2073	2082	1922	151	3	4
Terah dies,	3409	2070	——	——	148	3	1
Abraham called,	——	——	2083	1921	149	3	2
He goes to Egypt,	3410	2069	2084	1920	149	—	—
Covenant of God with him. Gen. xv.,	3418	2061	2091	1913	148	3	1
Ishmael born,	3420	2059	2094	1910	149	3	2
The Covenant of Circumcision; Sodom destroyed; Conception of Isaac,	3433	2046	2107	1897	149	—	—
Isaac born,	3434	2045	2108	1896	149	—	—

A COMPARATIVE TABLE OF THE

Names and Events.	Septuagint.		Hebrew.		Difference to the Christian Era.		
	Year of the World.	Before Christ.	Year of the World.	Before Christ.	Years.	Jubilees.	
						Jubs.	Yrs.
His marriage,	3474	2005	2148	1856	149	3	2
Jacob born,	3494	1985	2168	1836	149	—	—
Abraham dies,	3509	1970	2183	1821	149	—	—
Jacob goes to Padan-aram	3571	1908	2244	1760	148	3	1
Reuben born when Jacob was 78 years,	3572	1907	2252	1752	155	3	8
Simeon born, Jacob 80,	3574	1905	2253	1751	154	3	7
Levi born, Jacob 81,	3575	1904	2254	1750	154	—	—
Judah born, Jacob 82,	3576	1903	2255	1749	154	—	—
Joseph born, Jacob 91,	3585	1894	2259	1745	149	3	2
Jacob returns from Padan-aram,	3591	1888	2265	1739	149	—	—
He arrives at Shechem,	3592	1887					
Benjamin born, Jacob 104,	3598	1881	2272	1732	149	—	—
Isaac dies,	3614	1865	2288	1716	149	—	—
Joseph stands before Pharaoh,	3615	1864	2289	1715	149	—	—
First year of plenty,	3616	1863	——	——	148	3	1
First year of famine,	3623	1856	2296	1708	148	—	—
Jacob and family go to Egypt,	3624	1855	2298	1706	149	3	2
They settle in Goshen,	3625	1854					
Famine ended,	3630	1849	2303	1701	148	3	1
Jacob dies,	3641	1838	2315	1689	149	3	2
Amram born,	3684	1795					
Joseph dies,	3695	1784	2369	1635	149	—	—
Levi dies,	3712	1767					
Aaron born,	3756	1723	2430	1574	149	—	—
Moses born,	3759	1720	2433	1571	149	—	—
Appearance of God to Moses at the bush,	3839	1640	2513	1491	149	—	—
Exodus,	3840	1639	——	——	148	3	1
Tabernacle reared. Sin of Spies,	3841	1638	2514	1490	148	—	—

SEPTUAGINT AND HEBREW CHRONOLOGIES, &c.

Names and Events.	Septuagint.		Hebrew.		Difference to the Christian Era.		
	Year of the World.	Before Christ.	Year of the World.	Before Christ.	Years.	Jubilees.	
						Jubs.	Ys.
Miriam dies in the first month, Aaron in the fifth, and Moses on the 7th day of the twelfth,	3879	1600	2553	1451	149	3	2
Joshua enters Canaan,	3880	1599	—	—	148	—	—
Division of the lands,	3886	1593	2559	1445	148	3	1
Joshua dies,	3896	1583	2577	1427	156	3	9
I. Servitude.—Cushan-rishathaim,	3907	1572	2591	1413	159	3	12
Othniel judge. Rest 40 years,	3915	1564	2599	1405	159	—	—
II. Servitude.—Eglon king of Moab 18 years,	3955	1524	2662	1342	182	3	35
Ehud and then Shamgar. Rest 80 years,	3973	1506	2679	1325	181	3	34
III. Servitude.—Jabin king of Canaan and Sisera, 20 years,	4053	1426	2699	1305	121	2	23
Deborah and Barak judges. Rest 40 years,	4073	1406	2719	1285	121	2	23
IV. Servitude.—Midian 7 years,	4113	1366	2752	1252	114	2	16
Gideon judge. Rest 40 years,	4120	1359	2759	1245	114	2	16
Abimelech judge 3 years,	4160	1319	2769	1235	84	1	35
Tolah, 23 years,	4163	1316	2772	1232	84	1	35
Jair, 22 years,	4186	1293	2789	1215	78	1	29
V. Servitude.—Ammonites and Philistines, 18 years,	4208	1271	2799	1205	66	1	17
Jephthah, 6 years,	4226	1253	2817	1187	66	—	—
Ibzan, 7 years,	4232	1247	2823	1181	66	—	—
Elon, 10 years,	4239	1240	2830	1174	66	—	—
Abdon, 8 years,	4249	1230	2840	1164	66	—	—
VI. Servitude.—Philistines 40 years, 20 of which Samson was judge.	4257	1222	2848	1156	66	—	—

A COMPARATIVE TABLE OF THE

Names and Events.	Septuagint.		Hebrew.		Difference to the Christian Era.		
	Year of the World.	Before Christ.	Year of the World.	Before Christ.	Years.	Jubilees.	
						Jubs.	Yrs.
Eli, judge 40 years,	4297	1182	2848	1156	26	0	26
VII. Servitude.—Philistines. Ark at Kirjath-jearim, 20 years,	4337	1142	2888	1116	26	0	26
Samuel judges 12 years,	4357	1122	2908	1096	26	—	—
Saul, king 40 years,	4369	1110	2909	1095	15	0	15
His 3d year, 1 Sam. xiii. 1.	4371	1108	2911	1093	15	0	15
David born,	4379	1100	2919	1085	15		
Reigns in Hebron,	4409	1070	2949	1055	15	—	—
Reigns in Jerusalem,	4416	1063	2956	1048	15	—	—
He brings the Ark to Zion,	4419	1060	2959	1045	15	—	—
Solomon, king,	4449	1030	2989	1015	15	—	—
Temple founded,	4452	1027	2992	1012	15	—	—
Temple finished,	4459	1020	3000	1005	15	—	—
Temple dedicated,	4460	1019	3001	1004	15	—	—
1st Passover in Temple,	4461	1018	3001	1003	15	—	—
God appears to Solomon the 2d time, 1 Kings ix. 1—10.	4469	1010	3009	995	15	—	—
Rehoboam, 17 years. Ten tribes revolt,	4489	990	3029	975	15	—	—
Jeroboam in Israel, 23 years,	—	—					
Abijah in Judah, 3 years,	4506	973	3046	958	15	—	—
Asa in Judah, 41 years,	4509	970	3049	955	15	—	—
Nadab in Israel,	4511	968	3050	954	14	—	14
Baasha in Israel, 23 years,	4512	967	3051	953	14	—	—
Elah in Israel,	4535	944	3074	930	14	—	—
Zimri and Omri in Israel, 10 years,	4536	943	3075	929	14	—	—
Ahab in Israel, 22 years,	4546	933	3086	918	15	—	15
Jehoshaphat in Judah, 25 years,	4550	929	3090	914	15	—	—
Ahaziah in Israel, 2 years,	4568	911	3107	897	14	—	14

SEPTUAGINT AND HEBREW CHRONOLOGIES, &c.

Names and Events.	Septuagint.		Hebrew.		Difference to the Christian Era.		
	Year of the World.	Before Christ.	Year of the World.	Before Christ.	Years.	Jubilees.	
						Jubs.	Yrs.
Joram in Israel, 12 years,	4570	909	3108	896	13	0	13
Jehoram in Judah, 6 years,	4575	904	3115	889	15	0	15
Ahaziah in Judah, 1 year,	4581	898	3119	885	13	0	13
Queen Athaliah in Judah, 6 years,	4582	897	3120	884	13	—	—
Jehu in Israel, 28 years,	——	——	——	——			
Jehoash in Judah, 40 years,	4588	891	3126	878	13	—	—
Jehoahaz in Israel, 17 years,	4610	869	3148	856	13	—	—
Joash in Israel, 16 years,	4627	852	3165	839	13	—	—
Amaziah in Judah, 29 years,	4628	851	——	——	12	0	12
Jeroboam II. in Israel, 41 years,	4643	836	3179	825	11	0	11
Interregnum in Judah, 12 years,*	4657	822	0	0			
Uzziah in Judah, 52 years,	4669	810	3194	810	0	—	—

It is necessary for me to add yet one or two remarks respecting the foregoing Table. The years of the reigns and administrations in the 1st column, viz. that of "Names and Events," are the number of years in the *Septuagint* Chronology of each administration or reign, from which the *Hebrew* will be found widely to differ, though in some cases the differences are of secondary importance. Thus I make the reigns of Zimri and Omri in Israel 10 years complete, and that of Ahab 22 years. Usher makes the former 11 years, and the reign of Ahab 21 years; but $10 + 22 = 11 + 21 = 32$.

* If, with Clemens of Alexandria and Theophilus, we make the reign of Amaziah 39 instead of 29 years, as their copies of the Septuagint evidently must have done, which also, I am convinced, was the true length of his reign, then the interregnum was only 2 years. See on this point my Synopsis of Chronology, pp. 21, 22.

These minor differences arise from the years of the kings of Israel, being given in *current time*, not, however, those of Judah, by which the Chronology is measured. The adjustment of these reigns of Judah and Israel will be found in my Chronology of Israel, Chap. III. See Table in pp. 20, 21, of that Work; and as to the principles of computing the reigns and administrations, see the Preface to that Work, pp. ix—xii. It is satisfactory to me to add, that Mr Clinton and I agree to a year in the period from the accession of Rehoboam to that of Queen Athaliah, which we both make 93 years.

I shall, finally, inform the reader, that I deemed it unnecessary to carry down the Table lower than the year when the two Chronologies meet at a common point, since the whole Chronology, from B.C. 810 to 1837, will be found in my *Synopsis*.

APPENDIX TO CHAPTER I.

FURTHER REMARKS ON SOME OF THE GREAT ERAS OF THE HEBREW CHRONOLOGY.

I HAVE said, in various passages of this Work, that the Hebrew era of Creation, B.C. 4004, is in the Greek, the 2d year of Lamech, whose birth was in B.C. 4005. Now, if he was born on the 1st of Nisan, that is, on the very first day of the year, then the 1st of Nisan of the following year, B.C. 4004, from which I presume these periods run, was also the 1st day of the 2d year of his age. This, however, is not probable. The chances are just equal, that his birth was not earlier than the 1st day of the 7th month, Tisri, B.C. 4005, and if so, then on the 1st of Nisan, B.C. 4004, he was only 6 months old, and consequently it was still only the *first year* of his age. We hence see, that the great periods of Chronology, which have been traced, commencing in that year, and ending that of 70 Jubilees, at the date of the last vision of Ezekiel, B.C. 574, that of 305 Cycles at the fall of the French monarchy, and beginning of the great war of the Revolution, and the series of larger astronomical Cycles at the beginning of the French Revolution, 1789, do all begin to run from the 1st of Nisan, of the 1st year of the age of Lamech, although in the numeration of his years it is his 2d current year, the years of the ages and administrations being necessarily numbered in this way, in order to make out complete time.

The attentive reader will doubtless have observed an apparent discrepancy between two passages in this Chapter, wherein I am reasoning from the Chronology of the same period, being the Hebrew era of Creation, and in the Greek the 2d year current of Lamech. In page 10, it is stated that the year B.C. 1838, which, in the Greek Chronology, is the date of the death of Jacob, is, in the Hebrew, not marked as an era at all, whereas in the Table, page 20, the same year B.C. 1838, appears in the Hebrew Chronology, as a marked Jubilean era, 2 years before the birth of Jacob, and I have, consequently, put it down as the date of Isaac's entreating for the barrenness of his wife, on the supposition that his faith was tried by some delay before Rebekah conceived, which was in the following year. It was, at any rate, the last year of Rebekah's barrenness. I shall now explain, that the reason of this discrepancy is, that in first penning my argument in page 20, I, from the mass of figures on my Table, happened by mistake to take a wrong date, and on its basis to calculate several Septenaries of Jubilees, and the error was not noticed till the computations were gone over in correcting the press. It then became necessary to remodel my argument in that place; and it was in calculating the series of Jubilees, in both Chronologies, from the birth of Methuselah, that I discovered, for the first time, that the year B.C. 1985, being in the Greek that of Jacob's birth, and B.C. 1838, that of his death, are also in the Hebrew, Jubilean eras. Before this, however, both page 10, where I reason from the latter date, and page 24, in which the former is mentioned, were in type, and it was, consequently, too late to alter the *forms of expression.* For let it be observed after all, that these two years being in the Greek, the dates of the birth and death of Jacob, while in the Hebrew, the one is the 12th year of Abraham, an era not mentioned in the Scriptures at all, and the other simply the year before the conception of Rebekah, both years do, as *great eras,* belong to the *Greek,* and *not* the *Hebrew* Chronology, and, therefore, the discrepancy in my statements is rather *apparent* than *real.*

I shall now also inform the reader, that since this Work went to the press I have discovered further evidence, founded on the series of Metonic Cycles, from B.C. 4004 to 1792, that the former date belongs to the Greek and not the Hebrew Chronology, for that series in the Greek divides itself as follows:—

First. From Nisan, B.C. 4004 to the same month, B.C. 1059, the date of the 1st Passover, after David placed the Ark of God on mount Zion, which is a great Scriptural era, as being a type of the reign of Christ in mount Zion, Psal. ii. 6; Isa. xxiv. 23; Zech. ii. 10; there are 2945 years $=$ $5 + 5^2 + 5^3 =$ . . 155 Cycles of 19.
Thence to 1792 are 2850 years $= 5^2 + 5^3$, or 150 ———

Secondly. Computing from B.C. 4004, the sum of $19 \times 17 = 323$ years $\times 5 = 1615$ years, or 85 Cycles, we arrive at B.C. 2389, just 9 years after the date of the confusion of tongues, B.C. 2398, and, therefore, in the earliest stages of the division of the earth, when the different families of man were probably beginning to settle in their respective allotments, being also exactly 63 Jubilees and 2 years from Creation, B.C. 5478; and thence to the year 1792, the era of the Seventh Apocalyptic Trumpet, and termination of Daniel's 2300 and 1260 years, are $11 \times 20 = 220$ Cycles, a perfect number, which again thus subdivides itself, 1st, from the year B.C. 2389 to the 1st Passover after the Ark was placed on Zion, B.C. 1059, are 70 Cycles; 2d, thence to 1792 are 150, both subdivisions being perfect.

Thirdly. If we carry on the series to 1868, being the year after the expiration of Daniel's 1335 years, we have 309 Cycles, an imperfect number, but perfect in its subdivisions, which are as follows:—

Events and Eras.	Dates.	Intervals.		Remarks.
	Years B.C.	Years.	Cycles.	
A. The 1st of Nisan after Lamech's birth,	4004			

Events and Eras.	Dates. Years B.C.	Intervals. Years.	Cycles.	Remarks.
B. The earliest stage of the division of the earth being 9 years from the confusion of tongues, 63 Jubilees and 2 years from the Creation, $21\frac{1}{3}$ of 12^2 from the Fall, and $12^2 \times 5\frac{3}{4}$ from the Deluge; and before the destruction of Sodom, the covenant of circumcision and conception of Isaac, 7 Jubilees.	2389	1615	85	Being 17 multiplied by 5; and, therefore, a complete period.
C. The 1st Passover after the Ark is placed on mount Zion,	1059	1330	70	Being 10 × 7, a period absolutely perfect. If, also, from this date we reckon a series of the *week* of 19 = 133, at the end of 8 weeks we come to the year A.C. 6, the 9th year of Christ. Reckoning once more from that date 5 squares of 19, or 1805 years, we are brought to 1811, the last year of the unbroken power of Napoleon. Or if, from B.C. 1059, we reckon by the square of 19, 8 squares bring us to 1830, the date of the last French Revolution, and of the death of George IV. and accession of William IV., which were introductory to the mighty events that have since followed.
D. The year after the termination of Daniel's period of 1835 years.	1868	2926	154	Being 22 *weeks* of 19, or 1463 × 2 years. This era is from B, 32 weeks of the Metonic Cycle, or 8 × 4; and, therefore, both periods are absolutely perfect. This interval is bisected by the year 405, when Gibbon dates the emigration of the northern Germans with 200,000 fighting men, who, in the year following, invaded Italy under Radagaisus.

Now, in the Hebrew Chronology, the dates B and C are no eras at all, the former being 41 years before the Flood, and the latter the 37th of Saul, neither of which are marked periods. It follows, therefore, that though from the Rabbis having stolen, as their MUNDANE ERA, a great epoch in the Greek Chronology, being the 1st of Nisan after the birth of Lamech, the sum total of Metonic Cycles from that date to the era of the Seventh Apocalyptic Trumpet, is a perfect number, yet since the filling up, or subdivisions of this number, are entirely wanting in the *Hebrew*, while they are perfect in the *Greek*, the necessary conclusion is, that the Greek is the original Chronology, and the Hebrew forged and corrupt.

Having thus vindicated the title of the Greek Chronology to the Hebrew era of Creation, B.C. 4004, as being its property stolen by the Rabbis, I shall now offer some further remarks on the Hebrew date of the death of Seth, showing, that though not marked in the narrative of the Greek text by any particular event, it is, nevertheless, a great Jubilean and Cyclical era. It must already have struck the attentive reader with great surprise, to have seen, that it is not only connected with the whole series of Jubilees, of the national Chronology* according to the Septuagint, but also by a series of Metonic Cycles, with the death of Noah.† Let it be observed, as a key to the importance of this era, that during the long period which intervened between the Deluge and the migration of the human family from the plains of Armenia to the west of the Euphrates, which, from the signification of the name of EBER, "*passing over*," probably took place in his administration,‡ the earth enjoyed a perpetual peace; and under the gentle rule of the patriarchs, a golden

* By the national Chronology, I mean the series of Jubilees reckoned from the Exodus, B.C. 1639, and reckoned either upwards to the Fall, B.C. 5461, or downwards to the liberty of Jehoiachin, B.C. 561.

† See above, pp. 53, 54.

‡ As his administration began exactly 798 years, or 6 weeks of 19 from the birth of Shem, it was exactly 700 years from the Flood, during half of which, or 70 × 5 = 350 years, Noah governed the earth. This was probably the golden age of the ancients. Shem might introduce the silver age.

age of felicity, from which, without doubt, originated the heathen traditions of such an age, which are thus shown, according to the Greek Chronology, to be founded in truth, but are annihilated by the absurd tale of the Hebrew Chronology, that Babel was built during the life of Noah. During this hsppy age there were no changes or political events to mark the succession of time, of which the only measure was, therefore, the ages of the patriarchs.

Now, the whole life of Noah, being 950 years, or 50 Cycles of 19, divides itself into 10 equal parts of 95 each, and the Jewish Scribes have fixed their spurious date of the death of Seth in the year B.C. 2962, or at that point in the true Chronology, when *nine-tenths* of the life of that patriarch were expired, and only *one-tenth*, or 95 years, remained, and therefore in itself a great patriarchal era, connected with the series of Metonic Cycles from the birth of that patriarch, and touching his death also, being from his birth, B. C. 3817 — 2962 = 855, or 45 Cycles. Moreover, this era also forms, as already said, an important link in the series of Jubilees, from the Fall to the Exodus, and the release of Jehoiachin, being the one which measures the national Chronology, beginning at the Exodus. I shall now place before the reader the *Jubilean* and *Cyclical* results, in the true Chronology, of the date with such deep subtlety chosen by the Rabbis, for the death of Seth in the curtailed Chronology; for although both these results have already been in part stated,* yet it will contribute to the more complete elucidation of the subject, that they should be brought together, so as to be seen at one point of view.

1. The Hebrew spurious date of the death of SETH, B.C. 2962, is, according to the Greek Chronology,—

From the Fall, B.C. 5461, . . .	51 Jubilees.
From the 1st of Nisan, after the death of Enos, B.C. 4138, ...	24 ——
From the 1st of Nisan, after Enoch's translation, B.C. 3991, ...	21 ——

* See pp. 53 and 54.

Also from that date, B.C. 2962, to the 14th year complete of Isaac, B.C. 2031, are	19 Jubilees.
To the Exodus, B.C. 1639, are	27 ——
To the birth of David, B.C. 1100, are	38 ——
To the liberty of Jehoiachin, B.C. 561, are	49 ——

2. From the Hebrew date of the death of SETH, B.C. 2962, the following results are obtained in the Greek Chronology, computing by the *Metonic Cycle*:—

It is from the birth of Noah, B.C. 3817		45 Cycles.
Thence to the death of Noah,	2867, are	5 ——
——— death of Shem,	2715, are	13 ——
——— death of Arphaxad,	2677, are	15 ——
——— death of Cainan,	2620, are	18 ——
——— birth of Abraham,	2145, are	43 ——
The 14th year complete of Isaac,	2031, are	49 ——
Thence to the death of Joseph,	1784, are	62 ——
——— birth of David,	1100, are 14 × 7 =	98 ——
——— 1st Passover in Jerusalem,	1062, are	100 ——

It will, on the other hand, appear from the Table of the two Chronologies, that not one of the last ten dates, and also not one of the former Jubilean dates, excepting that of the liberty of Jehoiachin, are found in the Hebrew Chronology at all; and if the reader will turn back to pages 53 and 55, he will see how defective and lame are the series of Cycles and Jubilees, which flow from the date of the death of Seth in the Hebrew Chronology. Having considered these things, I think no one, who is willing to see, can refuse to acknowledge that it is as plain as the light of day, that the Scribes have stolen their date of the death of SETH from the Greek Chronology.

I now proceed to offer some further remarks on the Hebrew date of the birth of ENOS, B. C. 3769. It has already been shown that this date belongs, on the one hand, to the Greek series of Cycles, from Adam's first year as a fallen creature to 1818 and 1837,* and on the other hand, to the Jubilean series

* See pp. 16 and 17.

in the Greek Chronology, from the birth of ENOCH * to the same year 1818. It is plain, therefore, that the Scribes have selected this date with an artifice no less profound than their era of the death of SETH. The birth of ENOS being, in their system, B. C. 3769, is from the 1st year after the Fall in the Greek, B. C. 5460, exactly 1691 years, or 89 Cycles, and from the 1st year of the administration of SETH, B. C. 4548, it is 41 Cycles. It is, on the other hand, from the birth of ENOCH, in the same Chronology, B. C. 4357, exactly 588 years, or 12 Jubilees, a perfect period. Now we have already seen (P. 38), that from the birth of ENOCH, in the Greek Chronology, to that of REUBEN, B. C. 1907, there are 50 Jubilees; therefore, by placing the birth of ENOS 12 Jubilees lower down than the former date, B. C. 4357, the Scribes obtain a perfect period of 50 — 12 = 38 Jubilees, or 7 × 14 = 98 Cycles of 19 to the latter date, B. C. 1907, and by placing in their scheme, the death of ARPHAXAD, (see the Table,) in B. C. 1908, the exact year of Jacob's journey to Padan-aram, according to the Greek Chronology, it follows that the year of the birth of REUBEN, according to the Greek, B. C. 1907, comes out in their Tables as the 1st of the Administration of SALAH, to which they thus have a perfect period from the birth of ENOS. Here, therefore, we have another example of the profound subtlety of these MASTERS OF FRAUD, whereby they have transplanted into their own system this important era of the birth of REUBEN, the first-born of Israel.

I shall now place before the reader, in parallel columns, the Cyclical and Jubilean periods which, in both Chronologies, are connected with the Hebrew date of the birth of Enos, B. C. 3769, and with this era, B. C. 1907, which is thus claimed by both schemes.

SERIES OF METONIC CYCLES.

Greek Events and Dates.	B.C.	Intervals in Cycles of 19.	Hebrew Events and Dates.	B.C.	Intervals in Cycles of 19.
1. Adam's 1st year as a fallen creature,	5460		1. The birth of Enos,	3769	

* Page 40.

Greek Events and Dates.	B.C.		Intervals in Cycles of 19.
2. The 1st year of the administration of Seth,	4548		48
3. *The spurious Hebrew date of the birth of Enos;* but in the Greek a marked Cyclical and Jubilean period,	3769	These 2 periods make the perfect one of 70 Cycles.	41
4. The last year of the antediluvian earth,	3218		29
5. The birth of Reuben,	1907	These two are 70 Cycles.	69
6. Jacob returns from Padan-aram,	1888		1
7. The last year of Joshua,	1584		16
8. The last year of the 1st Servitude,	1565		1
9. The 2d year of Saul,	1109		24
10. The 21st of Saul,	1090		1
11. The last of Saul,	1071		1
12. The 2d of Cyrus in Persia, being 70 Cycles from Jacob's return,	558		27

Hebrew Events and Dates.	B.C.	Intervals in Cycles of 19.
2. 1st year of Administration of Salah,	1907	98
3. The entrance into Cainan,	1451	24
4. The 2d of Solomon,	1014	23
5. The 21st of Solomon,	995	1
6. The last of Solomon,	976	1
7. The 2d of Cyrus in Persia,	558	22

EXPLANATORY NOTE.

The 3d period of this Hebrew series was inadvertently omitted by me in the argument of p. 16 of this Work, as I had not then seen it.

The perfection of the first period in this Hebrew series arises from the deep subtlety of the Scribes in choosing, as the basis of the series, the era of the birth of Reuben, B. C. 1907, and computing back 7 × 14 = 98 Cycles, or 38 Jubilees, fixing it as the era of the birth of Enos, and the former date as the first of the administration of Salah, which is the year after their date of the death of Arphaxad, seeing that they annihilate the second Cainan. Next, there being in another Greek Series, from the 1st of the administration of the second Cainan, B. C. 2676, to the division of the lands, B. C. 1593, exactly 57 Cycles, or 3 squares of 19; they substitute for this the less perfect period of 24 Cycles, from their own spurious epoch of the administration of Salah, to the entrance into Canaan.

Again, there being in this Greek Series, from the birth of REUBEN, B. C. 1907, to the 2d year of SAUL, B. C. 1109, exactly the perfect period of 42 Cycles, or 6 weeks of 19, they, for this, substitute their own imperfect period of 24 + 23 = 47 Cycles, from their epoch of the administration of Salah to the 2d of SOLOMON.

Both the Greek and Hebrew series of *Jubilees* connected with the year B. C. 3769, have been given in former pages; but as some eras are omitted, and as it will contribute to the more complete elucidation of the subject that they be placed in parallel columns, I shall now insert them in that form:

Greek Events and Dates.	B.C.	Intervals in Jubilees.
1. The birth of Enoch, B. C.	4357	
2. *The Hebrew spurious date of the birth of Enos.*	3769	12
3. The birth of Reuben,	1907	38
4. The 27th of the Exodus,	1613	6
5. Othniel's administration,	1564	1
6. Abimelech's administration,	1319	5
7. The last year of the 7th Servitude when the Ark was at Kirjath-jearim, being the year before the great victory of Samuel at Mizpeh, the beginning of Samuel's administration,	1123	4
8. The 3d year of the building of the Temple,	1025	2
9. The foundation of the Second Temple in the 2d of Cyrus,	535	10

Hebrew Events and Dates.	B.C.	Intervals in Jubilees.	Remarks
1. The birth of Enos,	3769		
2. The birth of Shem,	2446	27	These 3 periods are 38 Jubilees, or 98 Cycles.
3. The Flood,	2348	2	
4. The administration of Salah,	1907	9	
5. Jacob goes to Padan-aram,	1760	3	From the administration of Salah are 28 Jubilees, or 4 Cubes of 7.
6. The foundation of the Second Temple,	535	25	

It has already been said, that the series of time from the Hebrew date of the birth of Enos, is the master-piece of the Jewish Scribes; but it now clearly appears that its perfection arises solely from their having selected as its basis the two great Cyclical and Jubilean periods of the Greek Chronology, already mentioned as the basis of the Cyclical series, viz. B.C. 3769 and 1907. In fact, it will be found that the Jews have fixed nearly all the great eras of the curtailed and corrupted Chronology at the leading dates of the Greek, or original Chronology, as will be at once seen by the following enumeration:—

Hebrew Eras,	The Greek eras with which they correspond in date.	DATES. Years B.C.
The Creation,	The 1st of Nisan after the birth of Lamech,	4004
Enos born,	12 Jubilees after the birth of Enoch; 89 Cycles of 19 from the 1st of Nisan after the Fall; 38 Jubilees, or 98 Cycles, before the birth of Reuben,	3769
Methuselah born,	Japhet born,	3317
Seth dies,	24 Jubilees from the 1st of Nisan, after the death of Enos, in B.C. 4139, and 27 Jubilees before the Exodus, B.C. 1639. Also 45 Cycles of 19 from the birth of Noah, and 5 before his death,	2962
Lamech dies,	6 years before the death of Peleg, when he was 333 years complete, 6 Jubilees before the birth of Ishmael, B.C. 2059, and 27 Jubilees before the accession of Solomon, B.C. 1030,	2353
The Flood,	41 Jubilees from the birth of Enoch, B.C. 4357,	2348
Noah leaves the Ark;—Arphaxad conceived,	Death of Peleg,	2347
Arphaxad dies,	Jacob goes to Padan-aram,	1908
Eber born,	39 Jubilees from the birth of Methuselah, B.C. 4192, and 11 below that of Eber, B.C. 2820,	2281

		Dates. Years B.C.
Abraham in his 12th year; a great Jubilean era. (See page 20),	The birth of Jacob,	1985
The year before Rebekah conceived; a great Jubilean era. Ibid.,	The death of Jacob,	1838
Jacob goes to Padan-aram,	53 Jubilees from the birth of Enoch, B.C. 4357, and 3 from that of Reuben, B.C. 1907,	1760

It is thus made evident as the light of day, that all the great Jubilean series which are found in the Hebrew Chronology, are the result of this most profligate and most complicated system of fraud, whereby the Rabbis have transferred to their own corrupted Chronology the great leading eras of the Chronology of the Scriptures, it being demonstrated also, by the higher perfection of the series which everywhere result from the Greek Chronology, that it is the original of which the dates have been transferred to the Hebrew, and not those of the Hebrew to the Greek; for an example of which higher perfection, the reader is requested again to compare the Greek series of the Metonic Cycle from the birth of Enos, given in pages 17 and 18, with that from the same event in the Hebrew Chronology, which is placed before him in this Appendix, pp. 116, 117.

When I began the investigations imbodied in this Work, deeply and unalterably as I was convinced of the cunning and subtlety of the Hebrew Scribes, yet this part of their system of masterly fraud was unknown to me, but has gradually opened itself to my mind in the laborious process of analysis which I have been compelled to enter upon, I must say, by the reluctance of men on *this subject* to listen to argument, for, with respect to the Chronology, many, even of the true disciples of Christ, are either inaccessible to evidence, or unwilling to bend to it.

APPENDIX TO CHAPTER II.

ON THE GREAT PERIOD OF GEOMETRICAL PROPORTION FROM THE BIRTH OF SHEM, B.C. 3315, TO THE YEAR 1838, BEING 5152 YEARS.

It is erroneously said by me in page 91, that this great period is not a multiple of any of the perfect numbers, and by this mistake I have greatly diminished the force of my own argument.* I now find it is the perfect number $7 \times 23 = 161 \times 4 = 644 \times 8 = 5152$ years, or 7 multiplied by three other numbers, two of which, 4 and 8, are perfect. This number, therefore, is in all respects most perfect, and 7 multiples of it, or $161 \times 7 = 1127$, are exactly 23 Jubilees.

Applying to history a series of its *first term* of geometrical progression, or 161, the following results are obtained:—

	Years B.C.
1. At the end of $161 \times 6 = 966$ years, it arrives at the 1st Jubilee after the beginning of the division of the earth, 55 Jubilees from the birth of Enos, B.C. 5044, being	2349
2. Thence $161 \times 3 = 483$ years, end in the 29th year of Joseph, or when he was 28 complete, and 2 years before he stood in the presence of Pharaoh, being also Isaac's last year,	1866
3. Thence 4 multiples of $161 = 644$ years, lead us to the beginning of the 6th Servitude under the Philistines, about the time of the birth of Samson, ...	1222

---

* I am myself unable to account for this mistake; but by supposing that, in dividing the period by 49 or 7, I erred in a figure.

	Years B.C.
4. Thence 161 years, being from Shem 14 multiples of the number, or 46 Jubilees, arrive at the year before David brought the Ark from Kirjath-jearim to mount Zion, or the last of its remaining at Kirjath, ...	1061
5. Thence 161 × 2 = 322, being the bisection of the whole period from Shem to 1838, and the 5th term of the series of geometrical progression, bring us, as already said, to the 1st Passover after the captivity of the Transjordanite tribes, .	739
	After Christ.
6. Thence 5 multiples of 161, being from Shem 21, or 69 Jubilees, and 23 Jubilees from the last year of the Ark at Kirjath, end in the year when Vespasian, with the Roman army, consisting of 60,000 men, entered Galilee, . .	67
7. Thence 4 multiples of 161, being from Shem 5 × 5 = 25, end at the date of the final overthrow of the kingdom of the Visigoths in Spain by the arms of the Saracens, at the battle of Xeres, whence, to the *present year*, are 23 Jubilees, or 7 multiples of 161, ...	711
8. 1 other multiple, or 26 from Shem, brings us to the 2d year of the reign of Alfred, ...	872
9. 30 multiples of 161 from Shem, being 14, or 46 Jubilees, from the 1st year of the captivity of the tribes beyond Jordan, end in the year when Zuinglius began to preach, in which event the Reformation commenced, whence, to 1838, are 2 multiples of 161, or 46 Septenaries of years, .	1516

This stupendous series of time does, therefore, bring the whole of these *nine great eras* into chronological connexion with the year 1838, and the series of geometrical progression, the 6th term of which leads to this year, marks it as the point of fulness of the whole of these periods, which ought, therefore, to be added to the Table of great periods terminating in 1838. Were we to carry on the series one other term, it becomes 10,304 years, and leads to the year of Christ 6990.

Fullarton & Co. Printers, Glasgow.

WORKS PUBLISHED BY THE SAME AUTHOR,

AND MAY BE HAD OF

THOMAS CADELL, HATCHARD and SON, and JAMES NISBET, London; WILLIAM WHYTE & Co., and WILLIAM INNES, Edinburgh; JOHN ROBERTSON & Co., Dublin; JOHN SMITH and SON, Glasgow.

1. A DISSERTATION on the SEALS and TRUMPETS of the APOCALYPSE, and the Prophetical period of Twelve Hundred and Sixty Years. Third Edition, corrected and enlarged.—Price 14s.; or with the Supplement, 15s.

2. LETTERS and ESSAYS, Controversial and Critical, on Subjects connected with the Conversion and National Restoration of Israel, first published in the Jewish Expositor.—Price 8s.

3. The CHURCH of ROME the APOSTACY, and the POPE the MAN of SIN and SON of PERDITION of St Paul's Prophecy, in the Second Epistle to the Thessalonians. Second Edition, with an Appendix, containing an Examination of the Rev. W. Burgh's attempt to vindicate the Papacy from these charges, and to fix on the Protestant Churches the imputation of falsely interpreting the prophecies of Antichrist.—Price 2s. 6d.

4. A REVIEW of the REV. DR WARDLAW'S SERMON on the MILLENNIUM; with an Answer to his Arguments against the Millennial Resurrection and Reign of the Saints and Martyrs of Jesus. Second Edition, with an Appendix, containing Strictures on certain Passages of Dr Wardlaw's Sermon on Civil Establishments of Christianity.—Price 1s. *Out of print.*

5. The PRE-MILLENNIAL ADVENT of MESSIAH DEMONSTRATED from the SCRIPTURES; especially addressed to the consideration of the Ministers of Christ. First printed in the Christian Observer, and now republished with Corrections and Additions. Third Edition, with a Preface, containing Strictures on a Tract entitled, "The Time of Christ's Second Coming identified with the Day of Judgment."—Price 1s.

6. The DOCTRINE of the MILLENNIAL ADVENT and REIGN of MESSIAH Vindicated from the Objections of the Edinburgh Theological Magazine. With an Appendix, containing Remarks on Dr Hamilton's recent Works on Millenarianism.—N. B. This Work is at present *out of print.*

7. STRICTURES on Mr FRERE'S Pamphlet on the General Structure of the Apocalypse; being an Appendix to the Scheme of Prophetical Arrangement of the Rev. Edward Irving and Mr Frere, critically examined.—Price 1s.

8. A CRITICAL EXAMINATION of some of the Fundamental Principles of the Rev. George Stanley Faber's Sacred Calendar of Prophecy, with an Answer to his Arguments against the Millennial Advent and Reign of Messiah.—Price 6s. This Work is also at present *out of print.*

9. STRICTURES on certain leading Positions and Interpretations of the Rev. Edward Irving's Lectures on the Apocalypse; with Observations on the True Principles of Apocalyptic Arrangement and Interpretation.—Price 3s.

10. STRICTURES on the Rev. S. R. MAITLAND'S four Pamphlets on Prophecy, and in Vindication of the Protestant Principles of Prophetic Interpretation.—Price 2s.

11. The **JUBILEAN CHRONOLOGY** of the **SEVENTH TRUMPET** of the **APOCALYPSE**, and the Judgment of the Ancient of Days, Daniel vii. 9. With a brief account of the Discoveries of Mons. de Cheseaux, as to the great Astronomical Cycles of 2300 and 1260 years, and their difference 1040 years.—Price 2s.

12. A **LETTER** to the **EDITOR** of the **INVESTIGATOR**, being Strictures on his Review of the Jubilean Chronology, in the Investigator for May, 1834; and on the Arguments of Maramensis in the same Number, Palliating the Idolatry and the Abominations of Rome Papal.—Price 1s. 6d.

13. **THE POLITICAL DESTINY OF THE EARTH** as Revealed in the **BIBLE**. Second Edition, enlarged.—Price 6d.

14. **THE CHRONOLOGY OF ISRAEL AND THE JEWS**, from the Exodus to the Destruction of Jerusalem by the Romans. With Remarks on the Systems of former Chronographers.—Price 6s.

15. **THE FULNESS OF THE TIMES**; being an Analysis of the Chronology of the Seventy. In Two Parts. With an Introductory Dissertation, wherein are established the Epoch of the Fall of Adam, and its Chronological connexion with the great Eras of the World, and with the Present Times; containing also Strictures on the Rev. E. Bickersteth's Scheme of Scripture Chronology.—Price 12s.

N.B.—**THE INTRODUCTORY DISSERTATION** may be had separately.—Price 1s.

16. A **SYNOPSIS OF CHRONOLOGY**, from the **ERA OF CREATION**, according to the **SEPTUAGINT**, to the year 1837. With a Discourse on the Astronomical Principles of the Scriptural Times, showing that they comprehend a Complex Harmony of deeply Scientific order and arrangement, demonstrating their exact truth, and evincing that their Author is the Omniscient Creator.

17. **A SUPPLEMENT TO A DISSERTATION ON THE SEALS AND TRUMPETS OF THE APOCALYPSE**, and the Prophetical Period of Twelve Hundred and Sixty Years.—Price 3s.

CPSIA information can be obtained
at www.ICGtesting.com
Printed in the USA
BVHW041830180819
556168BV00006B/177/P

9 781377 279220